MASADA'S

MARINE

Judy Howard

Other Books by Judy Howard
The Cat And The Ghost Series
COAST TO COAST WITH A CAT AND A GHOST
GOING HOME WITH A CAT AND A GHOST

ISBN-10: 1480142425
ISBN-13: 9781480142428
Library of Congress Control Number: 2014907369
CreateSpace Independent Pulishing Platform
North Charleston, South Carolina

ABOUT THE COVER

The Golden Retriever's paw belongs to Captain Jack Sparrow, and the human "paw" to Robert Chadwick, both from Chadwick's Golden Retrievers of Hemet, California.

The Marine Corps ring was donated by Marine veteran, Jack Pleasant and the uniform by Marine veteran, Ron Gervais, both of Sun City, California.

ACKNOWLEDGEMENTS

Masada's Marine was a difficult book to write. It covers sensitive, and at times, heart wrenching subjects. During the two years of this book's creation I was honored to meet many people who continue to donate their time, money, and mainly their hearts in order to bring attention to the serious issue of PTSD. I want to offer my humble and deep felt appreciation to Mario Borrego, Kevin Crowell, and Mike Pullium for the privilege of meeting you. Because of your bravery and sacrifice at home and away, I had the courage to keep on when the writing became tedious and I wanted to quit. Men and women like you inspire me. Thank you from the bottom of my heart. I hope I have respectfully addressed the subject and brought awareness to this Invisible Disease.

Over a two year period, I conducted countless interviews with the volunteers of many organizations, veteran- related and dog-related. These people shared their knowledge, enabling me to portray an accurate account of, not only this raging invisible war our veterans face when they return home, but also of the hours of training and money invested in the service dogs donated to them.

Thank you, Shari Duval, president of The K9s For Warriors, a real non-profit organization located in Ponte Vedra Beach, Florida, (not to be confused with the fictional training facility in the book). Thank you, Shari, for freely offering your time and expertise. Your heart is big and your devotion endless.

My thanks go out to Cat Zoyiopoulos, CPDT KA, training director and owner of the Laundered Mutt in Temecula, California. Cat, you and Mike provided me with invaluable information about the training of a service dog.

Authors need readers before their books are published. These readers are invaluable in critiquing the accuracy of the content and the flow of the story. Thank you, Kristi Zeiders. You are my friend and a great reviewer. I worried the content would hit too close to home for you. To tell me that the story helped you during this difficult time in your life, humbled me.

Thank you to Melissa Reyes, my great granddaughter in the US Navy. Thank you, Honey, for helping me find my Marine critic, Joshua Zane Altemus. Thank you Joshua! You saved me from embarrassing myself in front of the entire Marine Corps. Your critique was what every author needs and your compliment, "I'm surprised you aren't a Marine," thrilled me. Thank you and stay safe.

In the beginning of my career as an author, my list of acknowledgements addressed the members of my writing groups. I have attended several, but Anne Dunham, your Monday morning group in Hemet, California was my first. I will always keep a special place in my heart for all of you who held my hand and gave me the courage to discover my newfound abilities as an aspiring writer. To all of you, thank you. You have made a difference in my life and, as a result, through my books, you have touched many others.

Also, I was privileged to spend many hours honing my craft under the unforgiving red pen of Jim Hitt's Thursday night writing group. Again, I offer my deep gratitude to every member's honesty and patience. I would not be the writer I am today without all of your support and guidance.

I would be remiss if I don't mention the people in my life who love me whether my books are best sellers or shoved to the back shelf. Julie April, I love you. You listen to my ranting and ravings, my bragging and my self-delusions. You are a good friend.

To you, Sandra Brown, my best friend, my best editor, my confidant and my sister, thank you is not enough. I could not have written such a moving book without you. An author once said he was afraid of writing the same book twice. You pushed me to always write a better book than the last one. I love you.

Finally, thank you to all my readers. You are the ones who write the reviews and cheer me on. There would be no reason to continue if you were not there for me. You are the passionate souls who make writing worthwhile.

Thank you to everyone. You all have made a difference. It is my hope, by writing MASADA'S MARINE that I can pay your generosity and tremendous support forward, and that I, too, can make a difference.

Oorah!

A NOTE FROM THE AUTHOR

Before I began writing MASADA'S MARINE, I, like most Americans, never gave much thought to our American service men and women who serve and sacrifice their lives so that I may bask in the California sunshine, sip a $4.00 Caramel Frappuccino, and discuss the latest episode of *The Black List* or *Dancing With The Stars.*

When the subject of our military arose, I proudly stated my patriotic views and gave a blanket, but silent 'thank you' to all who lost their lives to keep me safe. My heart twisted in sadness every Veterans Day and Memorial Day. I considered myself an average American.

When I decided to write MASADA'S MARINE, I imagined it as a nice story about a puppy named Masada who grows up to become a service dog and changes the lives of two men.

One man, who began his life as a patriotic boy, graduates high school, starts his own family and becomes a gung-ho Marine. The young man has everything to live for until he comes home from his first tour in Iraq with PTSD and loses it all, even his will to live.

Another man, who began life as the son of a drug addicted mother, learns how to fight a war of survival on the streets and exists inside a life of crime. The pressures of the young man's illicit career takes its toll, and he ends up in prison, defeated. He, too, has nothing to live for.

As I penned my story, the characters took on lives of their own and demanded that this not be a nice story about a man and his dog. During hours of research and interviews, the characters became people, electric with emotions, and sometimes terrifying, like the firefight that promises only one victor. As I learned more about the invisible disease, PTSD, the story's heartbeat pulsed out of my control, like the disease itself.

Masada and her littermates, the real heroes in this drama, matured into valuable service dogs. They changed not only the characters' lives, but my life as well. I am no longer the silent American. I hope Masada will change your life, too.

Every hour a veteran takes his own life.

DEDICATION

MASADA'S MARINE is dedicated to all our fallen warriors who fought the Invisible War and lost.

CHAPTER 1

She lay on the hardwood floor next to Lance Corporal Alexander March, USMC, as he slept in the dark. An astringent odor mixed in the autumn air and drifted down to her nose. She lay still, but opened her eyes. The bedside clock cast shadows across the gold oak floor. She squinted at its green glow and listened to the Marine's breathing- the only sound – air escaping in jagged puffs from his lungs. The patio door allowed light from a flickering streetlamp to beat against the wadded bed sheets. She jerked her head up, ears pointed, just before the warrior's flailing arms and legs rustled the covers, and his cries pierced her ears. The stinging smells of panic signaled her to action and twenty months of intensive training kicked in.

Her name was Masada. She was an American Service Dog. She was a professional. She stood ready and would never quit. She would never leave her comrade's side.

The Marine tossed and twisted, unaware of the dog's wagging tail as she jumped onto the bed and pushed her body under his thrashing arms. She laid her head on his chest and pressed her body against him. The distraction woke him, breaking the nightmare's pull.

He reached around and cradled her. She shivered with excitement, needing him to be okay and licked the Marine's hand and face until the warrior's attention focused on her. When she nuzzled deep into the crook of his neck, his muscles loosened, and he drew her closer.

Whatever demons that had stolen into the room and caused him stress, slinked away like villainous ghosts, but they always returned. The blood-headed vultures perched in the ceiling's corners, and waited for the Marine to sleep. These brazen, black birds of memory were relentless, never holding back from the advantage his unconsciousness offered. This was Masada's first night with her warrior and the collectors of carrion attacked again and again, no matter how often she challenged them.

The warrior sat up and swung his legs to the floor. The service dog shifted her body and placed her paw on his thigh. The Marine's breathing slowed and he ran a hand over his shaved head, scanning the room. Outside, the world slept in peace, safe from the terrors revealed in his dreams.

Like a soundless dance in the dark, Masada executed her practiced routine throughout the night, going without sleep because she was an

American Service Dog. She was a professional, trained to be ready and never quit.

Sensing another wave of panic, Masada jumped down from the bed, faced the Marine, and sat at attention. Hands that hummed with nervous energy cupped her head. The canine's sable orbs locked, unblinking, onto the veteran's moist blue eyes.

"I'm supposed to tell you everything. But it's as if you already know," the warrior told the dog. In response, she pushed her nose against his arm and licked his hand. Her tail beat a steady rhythm on the wooden floor as she sensed the Marine's mind take him away from the room. Masada leaned into her warrior's touch while he rocked with tight, sharp movements. His hand shook. He stroked his service dog and fell into the abyss.

A force which Alex had no control over pulled him back into the past where, once again, he walked patrol. It wasn't like the walks back home in California with his wife, Sarah, down tree-lined streets, dodging skate boarders and joggers. Everywhere was fuckin' sand and rubble. The air carried a thick layer of decay. He and Eddie had been in Iraq a week. As they patrolled, Alex wondered if Eddie still smelled like the fresh cut hay of Oklahoma and he of the salty Pacific coast. They swapped stories, Eddie about the States, but Alex couldn't stop talking about the shit-hole of wind and sand where they were to spend the next twelve months...or less.

Eddie bragged about his wife, Tanya, his high school sweetheart and their son, Ethan. They were going to get a place of their own when he finished his tour, maybe try for a girl next. Alex's and Sarah's story was the same. They had dreams.

Alex's fingers combed through Masada's fur. His voice rose and fell as he rocked to and fro.

He had only allowed a moment to hope that he and Eddie would make it home. Then he crammed the wish deep down for safe keeping, so deep that, now, he couldn't get it back.

He told Eddie, "We're riflemen. Teammates. We watch each other's back. Our orders are to clear the area. Move out the women and children, farmers and business men." He reminded Eddie, "Watch everyone. Remember that farmer pretending to be friendly the other day? He was the same dirty rotten haji in a group of insurgents trying to kill us the next day." Then he recited the KIA statistics.

Masada leaned against Alex's leg and laid her paw across his knee that jerked up and down. She gazed at him as if she hung on every word. The warrior's boots, the ones he never removed at night, thumped, thumped, thumped against the floor.

Eddie had argued, "We don't shoot women and children."

But Alex reminded him, "You're a Marine, a killing machine. You're here to kill. If they shoot, you take 'em out. No matter what."

Thump, thump, thump. Masada's tail beat out a rhythm on the floor that matched the cadence of her Marine's boot.

Alex remembered how Eddie's eyes sparked. The killer look. It burned in the eyes of every Marine, fueled by the weight of the Kevlar, the security of the camouflage colors, and the soothing scent of a well-oiled rifle. He shook his head and said Masada, "Our emotions were wrapped so tight with fifty pounds of life saving gear, it strangled any fear. We were well-trained Marines, focused only on the thrill of the mission."

Masada's ears pricked forward, listening to the Lance Corporal's voice rise and fall. The warrior bent down and encircled her in a hard hug, burying his face into her fur. She sensed his desperation. "The memories, the nightmares, the flashbacks, they're just too much." His muffled words and tears soaked her golden hair. Finally, he pulled away, straightened, and took a deep breath.

"We made our first kill the second day and we high-fived each other. The thrill of the kill kept us up all night." Masada gazed up at her warrior, listening to every word. "We were doing what we were trained to do. We were Marines."

The months pushed on like a convoy in a haboob sand storm. Each month blew in higher drifts of ugliness than the last, yet time and the tragedies raged on. Alex didn't remember when he lost the joy of the mission and its excitement.

He and Eddie patrolled the streets, Alex always walking point, always taking the risk. Broken windows gaped from the concrete buildings, reminding him of the dead eyes of his kills. Fluttering, tattered sheets, which did nothing to repel the desert sun, waved from the dark interiors. The bombed walls crumbled as if large bites had been chewed off by some sci-fi dinosaur, exposing an x-ray view of the stark emptiness of the Iraqi lives. Alex pointed to a soda can lying on the roadside and reminded Eddie, "You have to be careful of cans. The creeps noticed we like to kick them as we walk patrol, so they rig 'em. They can be IEDs."

Alex stood up and paced around the bed, to the patio door, about-faced, and back again. The rumpled bed clothes absorbed his words and left only a whisper to the dog's ears. His fists hit everything he passed - the bedpost, the door frame, the dresser. The sound of bone slamming against hardwood accompanied his marching boots, creating a rhythm like the drums of a war dance.

As they walked patrol, he told Eddie, "We'll cross here, proceed on the other side. You know, to avoid the can." Eddie didn't challenge the order, knowing it was impossible to see all the cans because of the deluge of trash littering the streets. Eddie stepped out in front of Alex and when they both reached the other side, the two Marines waved to a ten-year old boy who came running up.

"Don't panic, just be ready," Alex said.

"It's just Yusuf."

Yusuf came around every day pedaling movies to the Americans, or bringing fresh baked bread to their unit. For the first time, the kid's thinness and unruly black hair struck Alex's attention. He and Eddie had begun to look forward to the boy's visits, a bit of goodness in a mean, dirty world.

Eddie had asked Yusuf about his parents and the boy reported they had been killed in a car bombing. His father, who had been an interpreter for the Army, suffered the Taliban's retaliation and Yusuf's mother, unfortunately, had been along for the ride. Alex admired the kid's moxie because the youth still catered to the Marines. He was a survivor. He wondered if his own son would grow up to have the courage to live in a world of chaos like this place. For Yusuf, it was the only life he knew.

The Lance Corporal squared off and aimed at the boy. "Sorry Yusuf, no closer." Eddie inhaled sharply, but the small boy, unconcerned by the weapon aimed at his chest, stopped and waited. He had done the drill many times before. Alex swore to himself. If he had anything to do with it, his or Eddie's boy would never have to live like this.

In the dark bedroom Alex halted his pacing and sank onto the edge of the bed. Again, Masada moved in, licked his hand, and nudged his arm. He pulled her close. His knees jerked up and down once again, regaining their nervous rhythm.

Alex ordered Yusuf to open his shirt. The boy had no bomb strapped to his chest. Only then did Alex dig into his pocket for the candy. He remembered how their hands touched. The warrior marveled at Yusuf's small, soft fingers as the boy grabbed the sweets. Would he live to touch his own boy's fingers?

Nothing happened that day, which only made the two Marines more hyper-vigilant. They continued surveillance of the Iraqi, who shuffled through the rubble which was now their daily lives. The two Marines dined with Yusuf's aunts and uncles and visited his school, handing out more candy. Another week passed. Always alert.

At night they barricaded themselves behind the thick walls of the Forward Operating Base. Inside their individual, cement cells of the windowless FOB, they slept in small chunks of time, their sleep constantly interrupted by sirens that signaled everyone to take refuge in the safe zone. It was no longer the thrill of the kills that kept them awake.

"It was a Sunday," he said to the dog. "When Yusuf ran up and, again, stood before us."

Eddie smiled at the boy and reached into his jacket pocket. Alex remembered his regret of not stopping Eddie when he omitted the search routine.

Again, Masada listened to the Marine's words. She smelled her warrior's panic, and nudged his arm, reminding him she was there. He relaxed a little, came back to the darkened room and rubbed her ears.

"The boy just exploded. Eddie went down."

Alex had staggered, thrown back from the blast.

"Do you smell that, Masada? I do. I still smell the burning flesh and see the pink mist."

The Lance Corporal rushed to his teammate. He shoved a charred body part, maybe one of Yusuf's small fingers, off Eddie's back and carefully rolled him over. Blood leaked from under Eddie's helmet. His buddy groaned. Miraculously, his fallen comrade struggled to stand.

Alex reached down to help Eddie up. His hands shook so badly he was ashamed to look his buddy in the eye. As they both stood on shaky legs, Alex's hands continued to tremble, and he had scolded himself. I'm a Marine. I'm disciplined, physically and mentally tough. He wiped the dampness from his brow with his sleeve. He looked down at his jacket. It was smeared with blood. Yusuf's blood.

CHAPTER 2

Alex's attention came back to the dark room. The musky October night drifted through the patio screen door. The breeze carried the buzzing of the locust. It startled him that he was at the K9s For Warriors Facility in Illinois, two thousand miles from his Sarah. Then he remembered. He had lost her, too.

The hint of morning crept through the patio door and assigned a greyness that paralleled his mood. The clock's green glow matched the nausea churning in his stomach. The shriek of a police siren in the distance sliced into his migraine-tortured brain like a scalpel. He didn't mind. He was just glad it wasn't the FOB's alarm. If it had been, he'd be scrambling to the safe zone to spend the rest of the night.

Back in California he had refused the meds the vet center prescribed. The drugs worked, dulling the migraines, but they numbed the rest of him, too. Instead of drugging himself, he willed his brain to be focused, to feel, even if it meant only desperation. Miraculously, he had squeaked through his first semester of college bringing him nearer his dream of becoming a police detective, but he doubted he could keep up his studies. The immature students, the teachers' attitudes toward the war, and the crowds were a strain. The emotional drain of his troubled marriage was taking its own toll. Tonight was a good night, and his first night with Masada. He hadn't thrown up, despite his heaving stomach and the piercing jabs of the migraine. *And I haven't plotted a way to end my miserable existence.*

He sat at the small table, his burning, sleep-deprived eyes dropped down to Masada's. Her sable orbs watched and waited. The dog had to be tired too, he thought. The warrior noticed that when he didn't sleep, neither did she. Did she know how difficult it was for him to go on without his Sarah? In the promise of dawn's golden light, the dog stood alert, as if at attention, ready to offer her paw.

He pushed Sarah out of his head and studied his service dog. Something had changed. Masada had been with him less than twenty-four hours but he felt safer, less alone. Like when the US rockets swarmed the airspace over the FOB.

He touched Masada's soft, golden coat. *The dog only wants my love and praise. She doesn't care what I've done, who I am, or what I can't do anymore.* Alex rose from his chair, picked up Masada's leash. She pranced at the sight of it. "Come on, let's get some fresh air." Outside, he wandered around the building, taking long drags from his cigarette. He gazed across the dimly lit cornfields. In the distance their stubbles glowed in the early morning light. Life is simple for Masada; a pat on the head and her favorite, stuffed animal completed her needs. For those, she worked the entire night. He remembered when, like Masada's, his own life had been innocent and pure.

"When I look at how you live your life, Masada, some of my best childhood memories come front and center."

Alex was seven years old, dressed in cut offs and a t-shirt. Trailing behind his older sister, Arlene, and his best friend, Kevin, they explored the woods across the street from their home. Full of youth and innocence, they stalked imaginary enemies and hunted ferocious predators. Arlene kicked up stones while Kevin whacked his stick at dried mud clods.

On Saturdays the three youngsters wandered the shaded paths through the Eucalyptus grove and spent the day discovering children's treasures like funny shaped rocks or a blue jay's feather. This Saturday the young group lingered in a clearing. They leaned on a fallen log while Alex dragged his stick through the dirt, writing their names. Arlene, the analytical one, turned to her brother and asked, "What do you want to be when you grow up?"

"We want to be soldiers." Alex thumped his stick against the log, the hollow sound landing in the carpet of dried leaves. He raised the thick branch, now an imaginary rifle, to his shoulder and aimed at Kevin. "Blow up things. Kaplooee!" He jerked back from the make believe kick of his imaginary rifle.

"Yeah!" Kevin fell to the dirt, clutching his chest. Kevin, a year older than Alex and the inventor of the ideas for adventure, primed Alex with his desires.

The years had passed and, now grown up, Alex gazed across the moonlit, stubbled cornstalks. Those long ago images - dappled sunlight on the log - the rhythm of the woodpecker's tap on the tree and their names drawn in the dirt- they all saddened Alex. Two decades had slipped by. It was true, he and Kevin had realized more than their boyhood dreams. They weren't just soldiers, they were Marines. And they'd blown up a lot of things.

Masada sat by the L.Cpl.'s side enraptured by the warrior's voice, as if she, too, were lost in his story. He leaned over and patted her head feeling a flush of foolishness from sharing his history with the dog. "Come on," he said. "Let's head back inside, Masada."

Back in his room, Masada lapped water and crunched her kibble. Had the headache's grasp loosened? He considered the contents in the hotel sized, refrigerator. He hadn't thought of food in days because rage usually filled his belly. He inspected the contents and removed the sandwich. Peeling away the plastic wrap, he took a bite. His duffle bag lay tucked under the unmade bed. He took another bite and remembered his Uncle George.

He was ten when he discovered his Uncle's canvas bag stashed in his grandmother's garage. He had pulled his uncle's unforgotten memories from the worn duffle - a rifle shell, letters, a Marine Corps ring and white gloves, and an old photo of his aunt - and weaved them all into made up stories of bravery and valor. He admired the Marine Corps Band in the Rose Parade and fantasized marching in the dress blues. Inside he found the Marine Corps manual on guns and military terms. The booklet became the doctrine for his dreams. He studied every page and memorized the Marine's Prayer.

"Almighty Father, whose command is over all and whose love never fails, make me aware of Thy presence and obedient to Thy will. Keep me true to my best self, guarding me against dishonesty in purpose and deed and helping me to live so that I can face my fellow Marines, my loved ones, and Thee without shame or fear. Protect my family. ..."

That was when it all began. Little Alex and Kevin no longer dreamed of being *just* soldiers. They wanted to be Marines. Alex wanted to wear the sharp, crisp uniforms, experience the Marine Corps' pride and purpose. He practiced saluting and shouting, 'Semper Fi!' as he walked home from school. His heart swelled with patriotism.

Alex's dad had bragged about Alex's Uncle George. My brother earned a Purple Heart in Vietnam. He rescued his entire unit during a fire-fight." Alex's only desire was that his Dad would hold him in the same esteem someday. His father died during his junior year in high school, and after his father's death, Alex's convictions intensi-fied, as if becoming a Marine would be a memo-rial to his father.

When Alex graduated at eighteen there was little money for college. The recruiting office was the answer. He could be a Marine and receive the funds for school. Kevin, who graduated high school a year earlier, had already enlisted, finished boot camp, and military combat training. When it came time for Kevin to deploy, Alex, his mom, and Kevin's parents, and Sarah and her folks saw him off at the airport. Alex hung in the back-ground, envious of everyone's pride for Kevin, as they embraced his friend.

Alex joined the reserves with the guarantee he would receive the same intense training as Kevin, yet still be near home to help his mom. He wanted to be a rifleman like Kevin. His mother's humble smile swelled when she bragged that her son was a Marine. Her pride spurred him on even as he disregarded her private, worried looks when she thought he wasn't looking.

In the waning darkness of the small room at the K-9s For Warriors facility, Alex leaned back in his chair and ruffled Masada's ears while she lay beside him. This night was empty of threats. Only the locusts buzzed in the trees. He spoke with his mouth full as he finished off the ham sandwich, "I was so shy in high school."

He remembered his tongue tied in knots the first time he met Sarah. Every day after school the smitten teen, trailed behind his affection and her friends, always at a distance, like a love sick dog. The girls chatted inanely about their post on Face book and swooned over the latest country singer to hit the charts. When he and Sarah were assigned to the same study group, he finally gathered up the courage to talk to her.

Alex wiped the crumbs from his mouth. The Marine Corps colors, had begun to emerge from the darkness. He decided to take a shower and stripped down quickly. Stepping under the warm jets, he tried not to think of Sarah. Minutes later he dried off and, dragging his duffle from under the bed, he pulled out clean boxers. He dressed as fast as he had stripped, shoved the bag back underneath and made the bed.

Finished, he scanned the room to assure every-thing was in its place. The curtains reminded him of the ones Sarah had sewn for their small kitchen and even the occasional chair near the table was similar to the one in their bedroom at home in California. Everything reminded him of Sarah.

His mind drifted back. During their study group his relationship with Sarah heated up quickly and they became inseparable. After grad-uation and before boot camp, they moved in together and shared a small house on the edge of town. Sarah fussed over him, always painting or crafting to make their small quarters a home. She sewed yellow curtains for the kitchen and on weekends they traipsed from one garage sale to the next.

On Saturdays, at first light, the couple cruised the streets so as not to miss any treasures.

Sarah slapped her hands on the truck's dash-board. "Pull over! There it is. It's perfect. Don't you think?" She pointed to a small stuffed chair.

He pulled over to the curb and parked. She peered up at him, the sunlight deepened the golden flecks in her green eyes and he smiled. She threw him a kiss and scrambled from the truck. Before he could shut off the motor, she had skipped away. When he caught up she said, "The flower pattern matches the spread don't you think? You won't have to sit on the bed and mess it up when you put your boots on. You can use the chair."

It never crossed his mind to deny her anything. In his eyes, she could do no wrong. When she left her clothes strewn across the floor he joked, "It looks like a war zone." And when she left the top off the toothpaste, he shrugged it off - no big deal. Someday she was going to be the mother of his children and he knew she would be a good one. Sarah kept his uniforms washed and pressed. She beamed on the sidelines during the Veterans' Day Parade, cheering when he marched by in full dress blues. Sarah made him want to be more than just the small town boy he was. She never complained of his weekends in the reserves, though she sulked the days before he left and cried as he drove off. He figured her attraction for him was based on his love for his country and his commitment to the Marine Corps. Or, maybe it was just the uniform. Either way, she was crazy about him. In a rush of heated desire the uniform usually ended up joining Sarah's pile of clothes on the floor at the foot of the bed.

As the months passed the Marine Corps taught young Alex to be a man. He recalled each phase of his training. The day they issued his gear, the bayonet assault classes, rappelling, and the rifle training. He learned to maneuver despite his fear. He learned to trust his teammates and to earn theirs. He became part of a tight knit unit. The months of brutal training ended with a fifty- four hour endurance test with no sleep. He graduated with top scores and so proud he thought he'd cry when they awarded him the eagle, globe and anchor emblem. He was a Marine! He would always be a Marine. Oorah!

At home life was simple. Sarah's job at Wal-Mart would fit her schedule when she enrolled in cosmetology school after he deployed. Alex worked as a mechanic at Bradley's Garage. His boss, who lost a brother in Afghanistan, supported the war effort and Alex's weekends in the reserves.

In the beginning, the couple passed their evenings swinging lazily on the patio swing, soaking up the California sunsets, and retiring early. Too young to realize time was precious, yet they devoured each other with a hunger borne from the dread of deployment and the long dry spell it promised.

They married before he shipped out. Sarah, her folks, Alex's mom and his sister, Arlene, handled the wedding plans with little help from him. The women shopped and giggled, content to leave Alex with his head under the hood, tinkering with his '56 Merc or drinking with his buddies after work.

As his deployment date neared and his bond with his unit deepened, Alex spent more and more time with his teammates. Every night they met up at the Ponderosa Bar and Grill. Drinking, talking smack and pounding fist. He couldn't wait for his new life to begin - his future - painted with valor, pride and patriotism. If Alex's lack of involvement in the wedding planning bothered Sarah, he couldn't remember her complaining. Full of honor for his country and the Marines, he was gung ho, ready to be one of a few good men. He was ready to make a difference and change the world.

Alex scooped up Masada's soggy, stuffed rabbit from the floor where she had left it last night. Her head jerked up like a jack-in-the-box and she popped up, her energy sparked the air. Unable to ignore the dog's enthusiasm, he tossed the toy the length of the room. He counted three bunny hops as she bounded toward the toy, snatched up the animal, and returned to a parade rest in front of him. The pink fuzz bulged from her mouth. The Marine scratched her ears, pulled the saliva sodden toy from her mouth, and threw it again. *Aiden should have a dog.* He recalled his son playing with Kevin's service dog, Diego. He had lost his wife to Kevin and his son to Diego. The thought twisted at his gut.

Masada was now his closest-friend, no, his only friend. He continued to toss the bunny. Masada bounced back and forth, retrieving the toy. His tension had eased, even the headache.

The wounded warrior fingered his wedding band, turning it. Sarah had wanted a simple wedding with her family, his sister, Arlene, and his mom. With the miracle of Skype, Kevin, still in Iraq, stood up as his best man. He dressed in full combat gear. "The FOB's always on alert," he said. His forced smile didn't disguise his eyes which darted back and forth in response to the muffled explosions in the background.

But now, as Alex sat in this dimly lit room the only picture in his mind was of his buddy from a week ago. Kevin and Sarah, face to face, huddled in his buddy's truck. The cozy embrace...

Alex's tired eyes rested on the only personal item he had packed from California, his wedding picture. Sarah in a simple, white gown, radiant, cheeks flushed with excitement for her future. She stood before her father, her finger tips reached up to wipe his fatherly tears as he gave his daughter away.

"I know you'll take care of my little girl, son." Her father's firm handshake turned the statement into an order. "While you're gone, we'll watch over her. Her mom and I know you will do us proud."

Alex stared at the picture. The words echoed from the photo. "I will, Mr. Fredricks, Sir. Thank you, Sir." A spark of guilt pinged at his conscience as the words gushed out, because he couldn't wait to leave, to begin his honorable new life.

On their wedding night they waded in the surf at Montana De Oro State Park. A full moon illuminated the tide pools with a blue-green fluorescence. Toes buried in the sand, they marveled at the waves' crests, glowing in the moonlight, the ribbons of water, like strings of lights, floated to shore and extinguished against the rocks.

Masada stretched out at the Lance Corporal's feet, laid the stuffed toy aside, and switched to chewing a rawhide bone she clutched between her paws. Her eyes closed in contentment, back legs stretched out behind her like a frog. Alex studied the dog. *How was this dog going to change his life and get Sarah and Aiden back?*

Alex heard the waves from his past crashing against the shore. "Are you ready to become a daddy?" Sarah said. He stared into her piercing green eyes. His chest constricted at the memory. He had stopped breathing, grabbed her shoulders and said, "Really?"

"Yes." Her haunting giggles from a lifetime ago pinched his heart.

She squirmed from his grasp. "You're squeezing too tight."

"Oh, sorry, Honey. Are you okay?" He released her as if his touch had burned her skin. "I'm sorry. "Did I hurt you?" He looked her over and laid his hand on her tummy. "Are you okay?"

Her laughter danced and skipped over the water. "I'm fine. I'm not sick, just pregnant." Her small hands held his face and her fingers smoothed his creased brow. "I love you so much,

Alex. I always will. You are going to make a wonderful daddy."

Alex breathed deep, inhaling the memory. He longed to hear her vow again.

For one magical moment on the beach, the world had been his. *Semper Fi*, he had whispered under his breath, but to his bride he pledged aloud, "I love you, too. I won't ever hurt you."

Six weeks later Sarah drove him to Camp Pendleton. Couples clung to each other, crying and kissing their last minutes away, before life changed them forever. Because it did.

Once full of vainglory, the Marine now slid his body down onto the floor and buried his face in Masada's fur. He hugged the dog, wishing for what used to be, longing to hear his bride's words again. Taking another deep breath, he pulled back and studied Masada. *How was she going to change anything?*

Words of the Marine's Prayer marched in the Alex's head; *Help me to live so that I can face my fellow Marines, my loved ones, and Thee without shame or fear. Protect my family.*

He hung his head. Alex had stepped off the big bird over twelve months ago, he could do none of that and couldn't imagine how he ever would.

The Marine cradled his new service dog in his arms. She wore a vest sewn from one of his own uniforms, with the words, "Masada. Service Dog. Do Not Pet." Before the dog came to him, she had gone through twenty months of intensive training. All she endured had brought her here, to this place in time. This was her job. *But how was she going to change anything?*

The veteran hugged his dog and her warmth gave him comfort. *Could she change his life? Maybe, just maybe…*

CHAPTER 3

Alex had come home from Iraq two months ago. It was late November and the emerald hills still enjoyed the coolness before the summer's heat parched them brown. He tried to remember how many times his and Sarah's friends teased them saying, "Get a room, you guys." The reunited love birds couldn't get enough of one another.

Four months ago his son, Aiden had been born. In Iraq, Alex met his son through the miracle of Skype.

Sarah beamed as she held their son. "Aiden Alexander March, meet your daddy."

He stared at the computer screen, his son's red wrinkled face staring back at him. His heart swelled with pride as he listened to his son's cries escaping a gaping, toothless mouth. He had never seen anything so beautiful. Everything became clear, why he was there in Iraq, fighting for freedom. He fought to make this world a better place for his son. He had never been so sure of his mission.

When he landed at the airport, and Alex met Aiden for the first time, the travelers in the terminal vanished and the din of voices receded. He gazed down into Sarah's arms as she pushed the bundle toward him. Sarah's smile spread across her face.

Alex's hands trembled as he cradled the small human being. "He's beautiful." Alex said as Sarah beamed at the father-son scene with watery eyes.

The sight and scent of the toddler weakened the new father, yet his pulse pounded strong with pride. Sentiment that had no place in Iraq, bubbled up from the deep hole where he had buried it. When his legs began to buckle, he sucked up his feelings and shoved the small bundle back to Sarah, but not before his own eyes watered. He feigned uneasiness. "You take him. I might break him." He had held babies in Iraq - Yusuf's little sister, for one, but here in the busy airport was not the time or place for wishes or weakness.

"No you won't. He's tough, like his daddy." But Sarah's smile shrank as he handed his son back.

Ignoring her disappointment, Alex grabbed his duffle and said, "Let's get out of here."

Turning to leave, they paused because a tight crowd encircled them and had begun to applaud. An older man stepped up and reached out his hand. "Welcome home Marine. Oorah!"

Then a couple came forward. "Thank you, Sir, for your service," the man said.

The woman with him gazed down at Aiden nestled in Sarah's arms. "Aren't you glad your daddy's home?" Then she met Sarah's eyes and said, "And thank you too, ma'am. I know how hard it is for you, too."

Sarah eyes sparkled, Thank you ma'am, "she said. "Everything's going to be easier now." She turned with pride to Alex. "He's home safe and sound."

As others approached, Alex clenched his teeth and scanned the smiling faces. He nodded as his heartbeat raced and his chest felt clammy. He pushed past them. "Thank you, sir," he said. "Thank you, ma'am." His face flushed with the heat of embarrassment as he herded Sarah through the throng of bodies.

At the truck, Sarah strapped the baby in the car seat and automatically climbed behind the wheel. Wiped out from emotion, Alex shrugged, threw his duffle on the floorboard, and climbed in the passenger seat.

When Sarah maneuvered the truck into the traffic and Alex tensed. Unexpected alarm surged through his body, startling him. As Sarah drove, he scanned the roadside and peered into each vehicle as it passed, examining its passengers. He restrained an uncontrollable urge to grab the wheel in order to steer the car away from the slow lane and the road's edge. His breathing increased and he began to sweat.

Sarah, unaware of his stress, prattled on, "I need to stop by my folks. It will only take a minute." Sarah exited the freeway and merged into the street traffic. "My folks will be happy to see you."

She pulled into the drive and Alex somehow gathered his composure. "You want me to wait here with Aiden?" He wasn't sure he wanted that responsibility so soon after meeting his son, but the thought of talking to anyone sent his pulse racing even more.

"Oh, no. You have to come in and say hello." She was already unbuckling Aiden from his car seat.

What was wrong with him? He felt like a foreigner, a stranger as he followed her inside like a timid dog. "They're in the den." She said.

"Welcome Home!"

Alex grabbed for his M11 which wasn't there. It was his mother who first rushed up and engulfed him in her arms.

"Welcome home, son."

Embarrassed by his foolish alarm, he stood mute, and stiffly hugged her. He gazed over her head while she cried with happiness and caught Kevin's eye in the crowded room. His buddy recognized his discomfort and shot him a compassionate smile.

Arlene, his sister, pushed her way in. "Hey I want a hug, too, Mom." She wrapped her arms around her brother. "Welcome home, Bro." She cried, too.

Sarah stood on the sidelines, cradling their son. Over a dozen friends and family stood in her folks' small living room, and more mingled out on the patio creating a feeling of claustrophobia. Kevin approached, raising his hand in a high five then turned to the man next to him. "You remember Dave? He lived down the road from me?" The young man reached his own palm up in a high five. "He just landed from his second tour."

"Oorah," Dave said and they high fived and pounded fist. Alex wondered why anyone would want to do a second tour.

Even Stan, Alex's boss from Bradley's Auto was there. The man stepped up, offered his hand, and said, "I'm proud of you, Marine. Oorah. Your job's waiting for you."

Mr. Fredricks approached next. "Welcome home, son. It's good to have you home, safe and sound."

Alex's mom stood by his side as everyone offered their greetings. When they finished she stretched up and whispered in his ear. "Your father would be so proud." She kissed him and he flushed embarrassed by all the attention.

At home in their small safe kitchen Alex enjoyed feeding Aiden while Sarah puttered. His son ate like a recruit in boot camp. Alex played airplane with a spoonful of food, but the copter only made one circle before the boy grabbed for the mouthful, even though strained vegetables was the menu. The baby giggled on cue. A funny face or a few fingers to his chubby ribs sent Aiden kicking, gurgling, and shoving his tiny fist into his mouth.

Bradley's Garage rehired Alex. Life was good. He rose at dawn, already awake from the nightmares. *They'll ease up. I've only been home a couple of months.* Every morning he ran five miles easy. Eighty-five degree days in California cooled quickly once the sun went down. At five in the morning the temperature had dropped thirty degrees. He was not in Iraq anymore.

One morning as he ran, a fire truck approached from behind and blasted its horn. Alex hit the ground flat and scrambled for his M16 and then his M11. When he remembered where he was, he jumped up, scanned the area, thankful the world slept, and finished his run. *It's only been a couple of months.*

Most evenings he met up with his best buddy, Kevin, and others from his unit at the Ponderosa Bar and Grill. They drank like Marines on leave, punching each other and swearing as they told dark, distasteful combat jokes that only they laughed at. Life was good.

At the bar, Kevin crowded in next to Alex, sliding his cold beer close. "Have you been to the Paintball Park yet?" Foam from his beer boiled over the frosty mug and dripped onto Alex's arm.

Alex leaned away and laughed, "Hey! Keep it in the glass." He bumped a farmer on the barstool next to him who wore a battered straw hat mashed onto thick curly hair, smelling of dirt and hay. The plowboy, in one sweeping motion, jumped off his stool, spun around, and squared off.

Alex's boots had already hit the floor and he twisted to face the stranger. When the farmer grabbed for Alex's shoulder, his fingers only grazed Alex's t-shirt because the Marine had locked the hot headed farmer in a choke hold. The barroom patrons froze as they focused on the immobilized man in Alex's grasp, who could only stare, bug-eyed, at the peanuts strewn across the worn oak floor.

No survivors! The startled patrons read Alex' murderous rage and guessed the stranger was going to die. They waited to hear the crackle of neck bones. A flicker, a voice, penetrated Alex's Kevlar consciousness.

"Stand down, Marine." Kevin's words filtered into Alex's combatant trance.

The warrior loosened his hold. The farmer slipped from his grasp, stooped down. He grabbed up his hat and hit it against his leg, a dust cloud puffed out from the faded jeans.

Movement at the bar resumed. Kevin laid an arm over Alex's shoulder. The farmer's face was flushed and stunned. The man was a local farmer, like Yusuf's father. Alex's stomach churned sour with shame for overreacting. Pressure from Kevin's arm steered Alex back to his barstool. Before he sat, Alex reached out to the farmer, "Sorry, man." The man clasped the Marine's hand and shook it. He did not make eye contact, pivoted on his heel, and exited the bar.

Lit up by a flash of daylight as the farmer exited, Alex saw the bartender's face. His two hundred and fifty pounds stood alert, ready to eighty-six Alex, but Kevin raised his palm and waved the barkeep off. "I've got this, Joe." Joe raised his brows, shrugged, and set out another cold one.

Relieved Kevin had his back and had diffused the situation, Alex returned to his stool and grabbed the beer. No harm - no foul. He had time for a few more. Last call always came too early, but he still had time to chill out and, anyway, Sarah kept the fridge stocked at home. He had only been home a couple of months.

The next morning Alex cranked the wrench at Bradley's Auto with shaking hands. An old timer once told him that the hair of the dog would cure his condition, but instead he endured the rat-a-tat of the air compressor like he had the staccato of the RPG.s and M32s. He kept his head down and avoided the boss's evil eye. He slipped out early for a break and downed a couple warm beers he kept in his truck's tool box. With the edge off, the shakes lessened and he finished his shift.

Life was good. He had only been home a couple of months. His mother remained in California after his home-coming celebration as guests of the Fredricks. "I can help with babysitting and Thanksgiving and Christmas dinners," she explained. "It's too cold back to go back to Washington anyway."

Arlene and her husband returned for Thanksgiving with their own announcement. "You're going to be an uncle, Alex," Arlene said, as she laughed and place her brother's hand on her small bulge.

Life was good. Everyone shared their gratefulness and relief to have him home. The day after Thanksgiving Sarah's folks lent Alex and Sarah their RV. While the family babysat Aiden, the young couple tried to reunite in Joshua Tree National Park - as if Alex hadn't had his fill of sand in Iraq. In the solitude of the desert he would unwind. No fire trucks, no people.

After a six pack or two at the campground he mellowed out. At night they sat out under the canopy of stars and talked about their future. "Maybe we should try for a girl next." Alex held Sarah as they looked up at the desert sky. One day he'd design their bedroom ceiling to look like this. They danced to songs that he sang a cappella and they watched John Wayne movies, ending up sweaty and twisted among the sheets. Still unable to sleep, he waited for Sarah to doze off before he escaped into more of The Duke's adventures until dawn. Life was good.

The last night's silence was broken by the blasts from the RPGs and Predators at the nearby Marine Base in Twenty-Nine Palms. The bivouacs at the base demanded his brain stay alert. Artillery thunder pulled like a siren's song and he yearned to join the action. The night dragged on, stringing his nerves tight and tying him into knots. The war games lasted forty-eight hours. During the day he ran, rock -climbed and drank. It had been a couple of months. He had to keep up his PT, stay in shape.

They returned home. He blamed the migraine on exhaustion and once again he longed for release. Nerves drew his muscles taut as if he'd come off a week-long mission with no sleep. All missions were like that. He wanted to sleep. There was no reason not to sleep. But he couldn't turn it off. He didn't want to turn it off. He loved the rush. *I wish I were back with my team.*

What the hell? Was he crazy? Did he have a death wish? Guilt sucker-punched his gut. Sarah was so happy he was home. He couldn't tell her he wanted to go back. *Could he?* Finally, he slept, tangled in the twisted sheets. *Had it only been a couple of months?*

With the pressure of the holidays over and his mom and sister back in Washington he figured he could concentrate on getting back to normal. He and his buddies spent their Saturdays at the Paint Ball Park. A hundred acres sectioned into life-like movie sets. One had strong similarities to Deadwood for the cowboy attitudes, another they'd named Kosovo. The adrenaline rush did not score a ten on the scale, but it felt good. After the war games, smelly and dirty, they refueled at the Paint Ball Park's bar-restaurant. Crammed in with other paint splattered ex-military and bad-assed civilians, they joked, rubbing elbows with the opposing team who had just killed them off. They made plans for a rematch the following weekend. He had only been home a couple of months. Life was good.

CHAPTER 4

Sarah sat at the kitchen table next to Aiden in his high chair. "I saw Kevin at the gym this morning," she said. The dark, damp splotches of pink on her sweat band proved she'd worked hard. A bright rose tattoo peeked out between her cut off top and her workout suit's black waistband. A neon pink stripe ran down the leg of the sweat pants. Alex's eyes left the tattoo and traced the luminous ribbing from her small hip, down her thigh, to her ankle adorned with a thin gold chain.

Sarah's voice rose over the cadence as Aiden banged his spoon against the metal tray and Alex's body jerked in reaction to each jarring clang.

"Kevin said you guys are going to the paint ball place on Saturday."

Across the table Alex pulled his focus back to the action before him. "Yeah. I love that place. I like getting the adrenaline up." He shadow boxed and made a funny face for Aiden who giggled at his daddy's antics.

"You've been there every weekend. There're things around here that need to be done. You haven't washed the truck in weeks, I'm ashamed to drive it. And that oil spot needs to be cleaned off the driveway. What about that broken limb still lying in the yard? It's going to kill the grass if you don't get it cut up."

"I'll get it all done. When I get back from paintball."

Sarah blocked Aiden's flailing hands while she shoved a spoonful of mashed carrots into his mouth. The boy's face turned red and orange goo oozed out from the baby's tightened lips and dribbled down his chin. Alex tensed. He watched the boy constrict his features, knowing what was next. The screeching wail raked across Alex's spine like the sound of stripped gears on his Humvee.

Sarah, undaunted, only spoke louder. "When you start school you aren't going to have time. It needs to be done." She released Aiden's fists and they resumed their banging, joining the boy in his tantrum's squall.

Alex jumped from his chair. It slammed into the wall. "I said I'll get it done!" In reaction to the clamor, Aiden bawled louder. "For Christ's sake get off my back! I had less grief in Iraq!"

Sarah rammed the baby spoon into the jar and sprang up from the table as well. Her pained expression irritated him. He knew her tears would come next.

He jerked open the refrigerator door and grabbed a beer.

"Really, Alex? It's ten o'clock in the morning."

He wanted to leave. Get in his dirty truck and take it to the limit. But he hated everyone outside these walls. People stared at him like he was some monster. But if he stayed…he was afraid to stay.

"So you and Kevin do a nice sweaty workout together? It's not the first time you met him at the gym, is it?" He couldn't walk out and he couldn't back down. Combat mode. Don't back down. Ever. He heard the rounds pinging. They whistled past his ear and he threw the grenade toward the source. The beer bottle crashed against the flowered wallpaper spitting a head of foam into the air behind Aiden's highchair. The missile bounced off without breaking, then shattered on the floor.

Alex came to. Aiden, no longer banged the tray with his balled up fists, but his little legs thumped against the highchair. His small lungs bellowed even louder, protesting the bad vibes. A ring of carrot mash circled his gaping mouth like a target on his red face. Sarah cowered at the sink, then spun around and pulled Aiden out of his chair. She cooed to him, wiped his snotty nose and started to leave. Alex grabbed her as she tried to move past.

"I'm sorry. I'm sorry." He wrapped his arms around the two of them and buried his head against her neck. She smelled of sweat and baby powder. Her rigid body trembled and Aiden squirmed. "Don't go," he begged. "Look I'll get everything done. You know I didn't mean what I said." He kissed and kissed and kissed her neck, and rubbed her back. Her softness returned and he loosened his hold. Pulling back, he made a funny face for Aiden and the boy giggled and grabbed his nose. "Hey recruit!" Alex tousled the boy's thin hair. "I'll take him, Sarah. I'll put him down for his nap." She hesitated, then forced a smile, and nodded.

Alex wiped the baby's little hands and face. He whisked Aiden off to the nursery and stood guard next to the crib, singing softly, until the boy's lids fluttered and closed.

Back to the kitchen Sarah dumped the broken glass into the waste basket as tears streaked her face. The rattle of shattered glass triggered a stab of shame, as if the shards pierced into his gut.

He took the dust pan and broom from her, set them aside and drew her to him. "I'm sorry Honey. I'll get the rest. Why don't you go take your shower?" She nodded without looking up and left the room. He completed mopping up the floor to the sound of the shower which stirred up an image that flooded his loins. Finishing quickly, he tip toed past the nursery and into their bedroom.

The faucet squeaked as she turned off the water so he reined in his desire to join her. Instead, he snatched a towel and stood ready as she stepped out. Her face was clean from the incident. They stood face to face. Her eyes filled with surprise, his with desire. She smiled and stepped lightly onto the bathmat. Forgiven once again, he wrapped her in the towel, pushed her wet hair aside and began kissing her with relief. She arched her neck and leaned into him. He inhaled her strawberry scent and easily swept her up in his arms and carried her to the bed.

"Aiden?"

"He's asleep." No, he didn't want to go back to Iraq. Silently, he promised, once again, he would never lose control as they both jumped into the fire burning out of control.

CHAPTER 5

*H*ad only six months passed since he stepped off
the big bird that carried him stateside from Iraq?
No, it was a lifetime ago. Alex had landed on US
soil, anticipating home and warm, safe surroundings. He knew how his blue eyes stood out against
his deep tan and his large smile caused him to
squint, as he recalled sweet memories of those
left behind. When his boots hit the tarmac, he
scanned the crowd for Sarah and Aiden. They
waved, and when they rushed together, he held
them in a hungry hug.

Alex had been unaware of the unseen attacker,
camouflaged in the crowded airport, cooling its
heels like a terrorist. It waited to follow Alex and his
family home. How could the Marine have known
what lurked on the sidelines? It was another war,
an invisible war, one he knew nothing about, and
had not been trained to fight.

Six months had passed since that day and now
Alex pulled into the community college visitors'
parking lot. His head exploded from the thirty minute drive. He was early, three hours early. Unable to

sleep, he had occupied the night hours reviewing the route he would drive, which lot he would park in, and where the registration building was located. He chose the widest road, with the least traffic, allowing him to drive in the center turn lane most all the way. He sped along, barely slowing for red lights. The unexplainable fear that he had grown accustomed to every time he drove, caused his white knuckle grip on the steering wheel. It threatened to consume him, but he stayed tough.

Ahead of him the Walgreen drugstore morphed into a heap of rubble, surrounded by insurgents with rifles. He slammed on the brakes and steeled against his panic. Realizing the mistaken debris was only a pile of asphalt, and the hajis were only orange cones, he floored the accelerator and the truck's tires squealed. He sped past the building. Emotional electricity prickled his nerves and rang in his ears like the FOB's siren on high alert. Logic argued with his fear of IEDs that might be buried along the roadside. Fear won out. He steered clear of the number one lane. Reaching in his vest pocket, he fingered Sarah's tattered photo, the one he had carried in Iraq. His trembling fingers touched the glossy, but he didn't pull it out. Her image formed in his mind and he came back to the present.

He had left Sarah back at the house. She had offered to drive him, but the last six months of her hovering insulted and agitated him. "I don't need a mother!" he'd said. His harsh words smashed her offer like crushing out a burning cigarette - another habit he had resumed since back in the states. He regretted his reaction to her kindness before his words left his lips. Like the rockets he fired in Iraq, his angry remarks hit their target and extinguished, not someone else's life this time, but a piece of his instead. He was destroying the relationship with Sarah, yet couldn't stop. For the last six months, everything she did, everything anybody did, pissed him off. They didn't understand. He didn't understand.

His finger rubbed the slickness of the glossy in his pocket. The sensation grounded him. He could see, now, the rubble was only a pile of asphalt the Caltrans road crew had dug up and dumped in the parking lot. The insurgents he feared - orange safety cones surrounding the mound of road chunks.

Frustration pounded at his temples and replaced the adrenaline's electric charge. He would admit to no one he wanted to cry. Instead, he shoved down the rising bile and somehow succeeded in keeping the nausea at bay.

In the college parking lot, he pulled into a space. Unable to pry his fingers from the wheel, he left the engine running. He glanced around. Right flank clear. Left flank clear. Assured no one lurked in the lot, he banged his head against the steering wheel.

How was he going to continue this miserable existence? But he had to. Sarah and Aiden needed him. At breakfast his son's stubby arms reached toward him, flexing his tiny fingers. Tears moistened the boy's soft, sweet smelling face. "Da da!" Alex had picked up his son, hugged him and set him back in his highchair. Gathering up his backpack and keys, he leaned in to kiss Sarah. Her kiss, flat from the hurt of his verbal attack, still stirred him at the same time her silence angered him. Unable to deal with his wife's coolness, he rushed out the door to face the demons his family did not know awaited him.

Now, as he sat in his truck, listening to the motor rumble, the migraine's enduring pain distracted him from his problems with Sarah. He was a Marine for God's sake, and he was going to be all that he could be. How could he fail now? He was stateside. This should be the easy part. Yet guilt filled his gut, because he yearned for the action of Iraq. His anger pulsed. He released his grip on the wheel, shut off the engine, and jumped out of the truck, his backpack in tow. He sprinted the distance to the registration building, glad he had decided to show up before the crowds of students began filtering onto campus. This way he could monitor the crowd. A bench near the registration entrance faced the quad. He sat, legs spread, lit a cigarette, and watched.

An hour passed before students began to trickle onto the campus. Two young girls entered the quad. Their easy chatter reached him before he saw them. Heads down unaware of their surroundings, they only looked at the ground as they passed thick shrubs that lined the walk. Occasionally the blonde showed the other girl something of interest on her phone. The dappled sunlight caught her hair, illuminating the featherlike strands. Their giggles sounded like the birds singing in the trees, yet their voices triggered another wave of irritation. The muscles in his jaw twitched. His fists clenched. He wanted to hit someone.

The girls headed his way. They took no notice of him. He didn't need a criminal justice class to know how easy it would be to overcome them, if he'd been an attacker hiding in the bushes. He could take out both of them before they could cry out.

He pinched out his cigarette, shoved the butt in his T-shirt pocket then dug down in his jeans for the pack. Pounding it against his wrist, he flipped open the lid, and pulled another out - his fifth since he left the house. He lit it without taking his eyes off the co-eds. As he inhaled the nicotine, he assessed their attire. Nothing bulky - tight in fact – skinny-leg jeans and tees that didn't reach the Levis' waistbands. You didn't see bare mid-drifts on the hajis. Still, the females had not looked up from their girly world.

"Did you see what she was wearing?" The lower red lip of the raven-haired coed protruded. She brushed back her slick, ironed bangs that shaded half her eyes. "I gotta get a top like that."

"Did I tell you last night at the club, a girl had the exact same shoes as mine? I wanted to die." It was Blondie. Her arm swung in exaggeration.

They yammered on as he sucked in deep drags of nicotine. Approaching the bench where he sat, they stopped, and noticed him for the first time. Their eyes scanned over him and met his glare. With flirtatious smiles they said in unison, "Hey."

He scowled, got up and strode a few steps away.

They looked at each other, frowned, and said, "What's his problem?"

Relieved they were put off, Alex checked his watch as someone unlocked the doors of the building.

The registration process went well in spite of the voices in his head shouting unreasonable orders that would have made sense in Iraq. More and more students flowed into the large room and the noise of the crowd hummed, occasionally peaking with sudden shouts. His heart raced and perspiration drenched his collar. A woman with white hair stretched tight into a bun and secured by a pink scrunchy, stamped his forms, shuffled his papers and slid them back to him. She, too, showed no concern for her environment, unaware of the stressed individual before her.

He crammed the papers into his backpack and escaped to the parking lot and the safety of his truck. Inside, he locked the door, slumped down and yanked a plastic bag from a bunch he stored in the glove compartment. He vomited into it, another regular occurrence, like the migraines, and another reason he didn't want Sarah with him.

With each heave of his gut he wished the migraine's pain would split his head wide open. He was useless in this state and knew from experience the severity of the pain would render him unable to function for one or two days, minimum. The darkness of his bedroom beckoned like an oasis in the desert. Sarah left him alone on these occasions when he took to hibernation, but he was certain she hated his solitary behavior.

He was incapable to help with Aiden and things around the house. He tried to help with his son's care, but more often, she didn't trust his temper, and frankly neither did he. He used to be the only one with road rage, but now she exhibited her own. Her job at the beauty salon that she used to enjoy had become a heavy burden. She constantly complained about her clients' inane conversations. Bad drivers and long lines put Sarah into a bad mood that lasted all day. Aiden refused to fall asleep alone and was afraid of the dark. She complained no one understood what she was going through.

What kind of life was this for her? She didn't sign on for this tour of duty. She deserved better and Alex knew he was to blame. He tried to kid with her. Sometimes it worked but eventually his own anger raked across a good moment like fingernails on a chalk board. He had only been home six months. Every day he swore he would get back to who he was before he had left for Iraq, but he was lost somewhere outside the wire.

When Alex returned home from registering he threw his back pack on the table, rushed through the kitchen, and slammed the bedroom door behind him. He collapsed on the bed. It was only registration today, and he was wasted. If he were going to complete the needed police force classes, he was going to have to get a grip. How could he finish one semester or one class? Who was he kidding? – Not even one day, if he didn't do something.

The bedroom shuddered when the siren blasted the quiet night. Bypassing conscious thought, and before his eyes opened, Alex spurred into action. He swept Sarah up into his arms as she slept beside him, "Stay down!" He dragged her with him to the baby's room and grabbed up Aiden, now awake and crying from Alex crashing into the nursery, "Stay down! Stay down!"

As he barked his orders, Sarah's shouts penetrated his brain. "It was just a diesel truck's air horn. What's wrong with you?" Her voice shrieked from her fear as she clutched and rocked the baby.

Alex came back to the present. He had his family pinned in a huddle in the hall.

Horrified, he tightened his arms around them, "I'm sorry, Honey," and buried his face in her hair. "I'm sorry."

She pulled out of his grasp and swiped at a tear. "It was only a truck passing by." Her words, cold and unforgiving, stabbed him. Still cradling Aiden, she stood, rushed into the bedroom. His body jerked when she slammed the door.

Sarah had begged for months for Alex to go to the vet center. "Get some counseling. Do something," she had badgered.

I'm fine," he insisted. She'd changed. She was always pushing. Just thinking about Sarah's attitude caused his anger to bottle up and choke him. He'd gone to the vet center, but it hadn't helped. They offered medications he refused to take. Instead, he hung out at the Ponderosa drinking with his buddies from Pendleton. They understood. Beer and tequila were better than any medication.

He crouched in the dark hallway. Look at yourself, huddling in the hall, your throat's so tight you can hardly breathe. You never acted like this when insurgent bullets hammered against the walls of the FOB.

He awoke to dawn's grey light which promised another miserable day. Rolling off the couch, where he'd finished the night, he padded into the kitchen, turned on the coffee and headed for the nursery's closet where his clothes hung. Sarah's filled their bedroom closet, leaving no room for his. He shrugged on sweats, and stormed out the back door to run five miles as he did every morning. The exertion kept him from keeling over the emotional edge on which he balanced.

He ran. A cold wind stung his eyes and swept the tears into his ears and hair. He pushed two more miles over his limit. Blood pounded in his temples as his boots beat a steady tempo. Along his path, he passed memories of body parts lying in disarray.

He returned to the house, spent, and collapsed at the kitchen table. He stared at the TV on the counter. He counted six fast food commercials flashing across the screen between news clips that announced last night's winners of Dancing with the Stars. White-hot irritation replaced the endorphins from the run and churned his adrenaline. The benefit of the run faded fast. He thought of the Iraqis who, on good days, survived eating only bread baked in their own brick kilns and rice from their fields. Now, with the ovens cracked and cold from the bombs, and the fields ravaged by American and insurgent troops, the Hajis existed like ghostly beggars living in rooms with snaggle-toothed walls and sun roofs designed by mortars. They dealt with fear and grief 24-7, wanting only for the fighting to stop and peace to be restored so that that they could mourn their losses. So many losses.

The kitchen felt warm after his run. The news informed him of the latest Mac Donald's sand-wich and the arrest of Hollywood's recent rock-star fuck-up. Alex hit the remote's off button as Sarah entered the kitchen with Aiden. She spread a blanket on the floor and set the baby on it.

He studied her coolness, and said, "Morning." He decided it best to say no more.

Aiden banged and flailed a wooden spoon on an old metal pot. His lack of dexterity caused the spoon to hit his chin and he burst into a bawling fit. His cries filled the room until Sarah scooped him up, and cooed to him. Alex squelched the order in his head for her to put the boy down, - quit babying him. The kid should suck it up, he thought. He shouldn't have been fooling around in the first place. Carelessness gets you killed.

God! What was wrong with him? He wanted to slap his own kid! Ashamed of his thoughts and more afraid he'd lose control he stood, "I'll be back later, " grabbed his jacket, truck keys and marched out again.

He heard Sarah slam a cabinet drawer as the screen door banged shut. Climbing into his truck he decided to tough it up, deal with the commuter traffic and visit the vet center again. He had to do something. He was losing it.

Last week his buddy, Kevin, had told him six months ago he had put in an application for a service dog. Excited about the possibility, Kevin explained what the dogs were trained to do. "They train them to wake you up before you have a nightmare. The dog knows it's coming before you do. And they say when you have to be in a crowd, they keep you calm. I'm not sure how the dog does that, but I'm going to get one. I like dogs. I remember the lab we had when I was a kid. When my dad came home drunk and raising hell, I remember how Brownie stayed by my side, like he was protecting me. Dad never messed with me. I think it was because of the dog."

Alex had saved the business card Kevin had given him with the counselor's name who had the service dog applications. Fishing through his barf bags in the glove compartment he found it and slipped it into his pocket. What the hell, at least he'd be able to go home and tell Sarah he was doing something.

The therapist was gone for the day so he made an appointment for the next morning. When he returned home Sarah's car was not in the carport. In their bedroom, the closet door gaped open. Only a few empty hangers dangled askew, like broken bones in a darkened cave. His heart lurched. He rushed to the nursery. Aiden's little outfits no longer nestled against his uniforms. Panic blinded him, yet he paused and sniffed his own camies that had hung beside his son's small ones. The smell of baby powder oddly put things in perspective, reminding him why he kept on, didn't give up. But the scent was almost too faint to detect. "Shit." He fled to the kitchen, found the note on the fridge and ripped the paper with the words he knew he didn't want to read from under the happy face magnet.

I'm staying at my folks. I can't live like this. He heard her voice as if she were in the room. Her resolve echoed against the walls they had painted together, a lifetime ago. Her words cried, begged, pulled at him, shredding his gut into a million different directions, worse than the damage of any IED.

He sank into the kitchen chair and stared past the warm, yellow curtains. He heard fire bombs in the distance. Maybe not.

CHAPTER 6

Alex rose from the kitchen table and grabbed another beer from the fridge. *I've got to get out of the goddamned fucking past.* He dug the phone from his pocket. He had to call Sarah, had to talk to her, plead his case, suck it up, step off, keep his head down, all the fucking acronyms. He punched in the number for Sarah's parents. Going up for report in front of his bad-ass lieutenant would be easier than what he was about to do.

He had promised Sarah's dad he would never hurt her. All he had left was his honor and that was whipping past his grasp like the sand in an Iraq haboob wind storm. He imagined Sarah hunkered down in her old bedroom, rocking Aiden and listing her husband's failures to her mother while her father stood in the doorway taking his own account of the cruelties from his daughter's Marine.

What if Mr. Fredricks answered the phone? He jabbed the cell's end button. His heartbeat raced. Maybe it was best to wait, let her cool off, but he thought of Aiden. He refused to be deprived of any more moments with his son. He had missed too many already.

He banged his fist against the yellow Formica table. The Felix the Cat salt and pepper shakers rattled out a clogging dance, their echo filled the room. Sarah had discovered the vintage shakers at a garage sale before he shipped out. Everything reminded him of Sarah. The throbbing in his temples matched the tempo of the shakers and made his head feel as if it would explode. *Shit.* He couldn't think. Anger welled in his chest and replaced his confusion. He would call now before Mr. Fredricks got home from work.

His mother-in-law's soft hello sounded slightly deeper than Sarah's.

"Hello Mrs. Fredricks. May I speak to Sarah, please?"

Her long pause grabbed and pushed against him like a tank crawling across his chest.

"She's feeding the baby. Just a minute." No small talk. No, 'how are yous.'

"Thank you Ma'am." He envisioned Mrs. Fredricks as she stood, her back rigid, her chin high, efficient, and straight forward, a no-frills woman. She would have made a kick-ass Marine sergeant. Suddenly, he'd rather deal with Mr. Fredricks. How had he not seen this side of Sarah's mother before? Mr. Fredrick's wife was the force to reckoned with, not him. He was no wimp, but if his wife put the mark on her son-in-law, Mr. Fredricks would see to it her wish was carried out.

His knuckles hurt from his vise grip on the phone. Muffled words and light footsteps came through the receiver.

"Hello, Alex." Sarah's voice was so soft.

He plunged in. "Look Honey, we can work this out. Please, can't you and Aiden come home?"

He thought he heard her whimper. "I can't. I need some time. You scare me, Alex. It's been six months. You aren't the person I married. Since you came back, you're a stranger. You don't talk, or tell me what's going on. I'm afraid for Aiden."

"Oh Sarah. I would never hurt Aiden." Tears that he was relieved she couldn't see zig- zagged down into his beard's shadow. He knew her response before he heard it.

"That's what you said on the beach in Montana De Oro. Remember?"

"Oh Honey. I'm sorry. I don't know what's wrong with me. It'll get back the way it was. I promise. I just need some time. Please." Silence.

His son babbled in the background, telling a long story to his Grandma only the baby understood. "I went to the VA Center today. I'm going to apply for a dog."

"A dog?"

"Yeah. They train dogs to help us cope with the stress."

"What are we going to do with a dog, Alex? Really?"

"You'll see. They say they help." He wasn't convincing her because he wasn't convinced himself. He knew he was grabbing at straws that swirled in the wind.

"Look, I have to feed Aiden. I have to go."

"Okay, Honey. I'll call you tomorrow and we'll talk some more, okay?"

"You need to get some help."

"Can I at least come see Aiden tomorrow?"

"We'll see. I need you to back off." He heard the catch in her voice. She was crying.

"All right, Sarah. I'll do whatever you say. Just don't give up on me?"

He hung up, slammed the phone on the table with such force the vintage shakers crashed to the floor and shattered across the linoleum.

The exploding porcelain thrust him back to a little village. He walked point, his teammate, Williams, to his right. They weren't scared because the Corps taught you to cram down the fear. It had been another hot, fucking-one-hundred-twenty-degree-fucking day, he perspired even now, sitting in his tiny kitchen. Fear, which never had a place in Iraq now filled the kitchen and rushed through him while more tears escaped down his unshaven face.

He reached up to wipe the tears from his eyes as he had the beads of sweat that day in the Haji village. He had been distracted for only a second, then "Poof!" like in the cartoons, when Mr. Magoo shoots the fence post and it vanishes into thin air. Williams was gone. The only thing left, the pinging pieces of metal bulleting against the hummer behind him …and the pink mist.

The shattering fragments of porcelain clattered to the floor like the chunks of Williams' gear ricocheting against the battle scarred hummer. The racket pierced Alex's ears and he thought they would bleed. He clapped his hands to his head and jumped up, sending the dinette chair screeching across the floor. He squeezed his eyes shut and twisted from the torture of his memory, but when he looked up, he saw his gunner's face. Their eyes had locked, they nodded to one another, and then, Alex simply turned and proceeded on the patrol.

Back at the FOB, with sleep a distant luxury, he spent the hours until dawn with his gunner scrubbing their vehicle of its red stains. The night that was never allowed to go dark, passed in strained silence. No dark humor about their recruiting officers' promises of getting some strange if they signed up, no fist pounding camaraderie. Each Marine swallowed hard as he rubbed away the traces of his fallen brother and thought, yeah, today was some real strange.

He hadn't given Williams another thought, until now. How could he have forgotten him? He rushed to the sink and vomited. When the retching subsided, he staggered to the kitchen chair and collapsed. He cried, haunted by shattered dreams and memories wrapped in guilt and anger.

He shoved the image of his M9 Beretta sitting on the top shelf of the closet out of his mind. He had to suck it up, step off, and keep his head down, if he wanted to get back to who he had been. So Sarah and Aiden would come home.

CHAPTER 7

Alex, once again, made his decision to, suck it up. He downed a few more beers - he couldn't remember how many- enough to allow sleep to come. Sleep rarely came without the alcohol, but when it did, the nightmares jerked him awake.

Before the sun came up, Alex woke, fully dressed. He rolled off the couch where he had spent the night and headed for the fridge. His habit of lining the empty beer bottles on the counter compelled him to count the bottles before he ran his five miles.

He ran to the rhythm in his head. "Ninety-nine bottles of beer on the wall ninety-nine bottles of beer. Take one down and pass it around…ninety-eight bottles of beer…" When he returned he showered, and with the edge off, he drove to the vet center for his therapy appointment.

Alex stared at the therapist. The man, in turn, stared at the folder spread out before him. The man finally peered up over his glasses at Alex and said, "You've been home six months now, how's it been going?"

"Great. Just great." Alex's voice squeaked. He tried to inject enthusiasm to convince the man he was coping, that the nightmares had stopped, that life didn't suck royally.

Dr. Why-Don't-You-Feel-Good didn't smile with congratulations but pressed on. "Is the medication working for you? Have you noticed a decrease in the flashbacks?"

Alex couldn't stop his knee from jerking up and down. He cursed it. And he blinked too often, his focus jumped around the room. The plaques and diplomas on the wall proved the suit had spent his life in rooms like this, had never seen a gunner mow down a mob of insurgents or watched his buddy disappear into a cloud of pink mist. He hated the man.

"I haven't been taking the medication but the flash backs aren't happening as often. My classes start next week. And I'm working on my 56 Merc." Fifty percent lies, fifty percent truth, the best he could do. He knew regaining interest in old hobbies was a sign of recovery.

"That's good. And you and Sarah? How's it going on the home front?"

The knee bobbed faster and sweat beaded on the Marine's temple. Were his legs going to get up and do a song and dance for this close-minded, son of a bitchin, PHD who had never driven a hummer in a hundred and thirty fucking degrees of gritty heat carrying sixty pounds of Kevlar and ammo and a tattered picture of his wife in his pocket while his heart raced so fast he knew it would explode in his chest as he smeared Tabasco in his eyes because he hadn't slept in forty eight hours? He wanted to kill the pious fucker.

"Sarah's staying with her folks for a while." His stomach tied itself into another knot.

"I see."

Alex stood up and paced the room. "She can't get a good night's sleep because I keep waking her. We thought it best, until I got back to normal. Her folks can help with the day care."

"You both decided?"

"Yes sir." Alex sat back down, leaned forward, and placed his elbows on his knees to keep them still. "Listen Doc, my buddy told me he's getting a service dog. I want to apply for one, too."

"Well, you're doing so well, why would you want one? There's a waiting list you know?"

The fucker knows I'm lying. "My buddy told me the dogs really help with anxiety. I'm doing great, but I think a dog would really help."

"How does Sarah feel about getting a dog?"

"She's for it. Anything that will help." His voice squeaked again but he forged on. "Sarah loves dogs."

"These dogs aren't pets, you know. They're working dogs. Just like the bomb sniffers. They have a job to do."

God, I hate this man. "I understand, Sir.

"I'll get the forms and information for you. I'll have them next week when you come for our group session. Attending is part of the requirement for a dog."

The fucker's going to make me crawl for the dog. "Great. I'll see you next week." Alex stood hoping the action would end this miserable hour.

It worked. "Thank you, Sir." Alex reached out and shook the doc's hand so hard the man's glasses slid farther down his nose.

He couldn't get outside fast enough. Sprinting to his truck, the vibration of his cell phone tickled his leg as he jumped into the cab. Digging it out, Sarah's face smiled at him on the screen. His stomach cramped in his gut and his heart beat with hope.

"Hey." A lame greeting. His insides twisted like spaghetti.

"Would you like to come over? See Aiden? Maybe we could talk?" He heard her voice quiver, glad she was nervous too.

"I'll be right there." He threw the phone onto the seat, shoved the truck in reverse, and barely missed a car pulling into the space next to him.

CHAPTER 8

Alex parked on the shaded street in front of the ranch style house, afraid to pull onto the inlaid brick driveway in case his truck still leaked oil. The Fredrick's home sat on the back of the property. From the front porch a red brick walkway cut through a manicured lawn and descended down to the street. The grass reminded him he was not in Iraq. Not one blade reached over onto the matching brick driveway. He thought of Sarah's discarded clothes scattered across the bedroom floor. Every night he tossed the items she had shed into the hamper before he climbed in beside her. Sarah had not inherited her parents' meticulousness.

He shut off the ignition but did not move. What was he going to say? How could he convince her to come home? He knew he was outside the wire. Vulnerable. He had nothing. He'd sell her on the dog idea. Maybe that would give her hope. And he'd cut down on the drinking. God! He's told her all that before. Not about the dog. He'd go with the dog.

He sucked in a deep breath and wished he'd brought something. Flowers. Candy. Something. His hands trembled more than they ever did after a firefight. He grabbed a brochure lying next to his phone on the seat. "Service Dogs and PTSD" He didn't remember picking it up at the vet center but shrugged and crammed the pamphlet in his pocket. That'll work. He swept up his cell phone and pushed against the door. Rubbery legs almost collapsed when his boots hit the asphalt. He drew himself up to full height, squared his shoulders and killed the habit to shrug the strap of his M-11 over his shoulder. You're home. He marched up to the front door and pounded on it with fisted white knuckles.

Mr. Fredricks opened the door and stood, reflecting his son-in-law's steeled, rigid stance. Their eyes locked. Alex's heart pushed against his chest like when he had to clear a building and prayed no one was inside. Now he prayed he wouldn't kill what might be his last opportunity to get Sarah and Aiden back.

The crease above Mr. Fredricks' brow softened, and he looked past Alex to his truck parked on the street. "Still leaking?" The man didn't smile but Alex sensed, or maybe only hoped, to find some compassion in his voice. His father-in-law was a Viet Nam veteran and Alex realized at that moment the man never spoke of his service.

"Yes Sir. I've torn it all apart and put it back together, and she still leaks."

"Well, some things we can't change." The man took a tired deep breath and pushed open the screen door. "Sarah's out on the patio with Aiden." He stepped back and Alex entered. Shaky legs carried him through the house to the back yard. His skin crawled. He prayed he acted normal. He stood for a moment at the patio screen door and took in the scene.

Aiden's childish voice babbled to the sound of sloshing water, his pudgy arms hit the water as he sat in a blue plastic wading pool. He splashed droplets of water onto Sarah's bare legs as she marched around him singing, "... if the Army or the Navy ever looks on Heaven's shores...."

Alex's guard melted. His Iraq history faded. Emotion tangled his gut into a knot. He didn't want to open the door, squash the sand castle setting.

He slid the door open and Sarah turned to the sound. Her smile washed away. Aiden squealed with what Alex interpreted as "Daddy," and reached out his small arms.

Alex swept up the dripping baby, a bundle of soft skin, slick and shining in the sunlight. He smelled the water and felt his t-shirt cool from the wetness as he hugged his son. The boy's tiny finger touched his daddy's nose.

Alex leaned back, ruffled the boy's wet hair and smiled. "You were playing Marine."

Aiden wiggled to free himself and Alex allowed him to slide down. When the little legs hit the ground, like a wind-up toy, they propelled him in a bumpy crawl back to the pool. Alex soaked up the tiny moment, stowed the scene away in some album in his mind and brought his attention to Sarah.

She dabbed a towel over her tanned legs and bare feet as she sat on the chaise, her hair pulled back with a clip. She wore no makeup and her pink t-shirt, darkened by damp spots, clung to her breasts. He stepped forward and grabbed her towel, "Here let me do that." He rubbed her wet legs with a nervous roughness as he tried to distract his body and remember why he had come.

Aiden squealed in delight again as he reached into the pool and splashed the water. Relishing the distraction, Alex focused on the toddler as the boy plopped down on his butt. The child's laughter rang in his ears like music, and his son's joy triggered tears that Alex pushed back. Alex turned away and pretended to cough. Too quickly he said, "Isn't it time for his nap?"

"Mom said she'd watch him while we talked."

He heard Sarah's irritation. "I'm sorry Honey. I didn't mean to be short. I just need you and Aiden to come home."

She turned to Aiden. "Come on little Leatherneck. Time for your nap."

The child's face squeezed in protest.

"Remember," she said. "Marines know how to take orders."

Sarah and Alex's eyes met, and they shared a smile.

With Aiden tucked in and his lids fluttering in innocent sleep, they slipped back out to the patio.

Sarah sat on the picnic table bench and Alex slid in across from her. He held his breath, waiting for her to speak. Her eyes moved across the yard, jumping from tree to bush to tree, then filled with tears that didn't fall. "I think we should take a break," she said. "You need to get a place so Aiden and I can come home. Staying here is too much for my folks."

Alex's heart slammed against his chest. A rage he had never known burned his throat. His eyes fell on Aiden's stuffed bulldog lying on the chaise. He clamped his jaw and spoke slowly. "Are you sure that's what you want?" *Dear God, please let her say no.*

"No." Her tears let loose.

His heart swelled up with hope.

"I don't know what I want," she said, "but it can't go on like this."

Now it slammed against his chest.

"I can't please you anymore." She went on." You don't tell me what's bothering you. Maybe I could help." She wiped her face and sucked in a breath. "I don't know what to do. Your drinking's out of control. You stay in the bedroom, sometimes for days. I am so worried about you, Alex. You scare me. I don't know what to do."

Alex, moved behind her, bent down, and wrapped her in his arms. "Don't cry Honey. We'll work it out. I'll do whatever you say. I don't want to hurt you. I want us to be like we were." He buried his face in her damp hair. "I swear I'll get back like I was."

He released her and pulled the brochure out of his pocket, "Look." He slid it in front of her. 'I'm going to get a dog. Well, I mean I'm going to apply. I'm sure I'll get one. They are trained to deal with vets with PTSD."

"Maybe I should get some of that training." She showed a weak smile as she dabbed at her eyes with her towel.

"It's not that I have PTSD," he said, "but they say the dogs wake you before you even have a nightmare." She was listening. He pushed on. "I have to go for counseling to get the dog." He knew she'd like that and he knew he could play the 'I'm getting-fuckin-better-game,' with the dippy therapist.

"Look, I'll get a place." He grabbed her hands and wrapped them in his. They were so small. "That'll give you some time. I can arrange my work schedule at Bradley's. My boss said I could work mornings. So I could pick up Aiden from your folks and watch him til you get home from the salon. That would help your folks out. And all my classes are at night. You and I, we're a team. Semper Fi! Right? We'll work it out." He took a deep breath. There it was. The pitch for his life.

Her eyes widened just a little and, once again, filled with hope and trust. He couldn't disappoint her again. It would devastate her. And that would kill him. He could not hurt her anymore.

"Okay. We'll try," she said.

He was back under the wire. Maybe.

CHAPTER 9

Alex left Sarah at her folks' house and maneuvered his way through traffic back across town. He focused on his own lane, resisting the urge to swerve. He kept a distance from every pedestrian he passed. Parking in the carport, he gave in to the impulse to search their storage compartments. He unlocked the padlocks and justified the search by telling himself he needed to take inventory of his things in case he had to move out entirely...if it came to that. Nothing disturbed, no IEDs, everything neatly stacked on his side of the compartment, but on Sarah's side, an assortment of odd- sized boxes some half open, sat askew and ready to topple. His eyes followed the disarray to the top container which overflowed with sweats, outdated outfits, and maternity clothes. Its cardboard flaps gaped open, unable to close. He cringed. The Marine Corps had engrained in him that orderliness was next to Godliness. He tried to smile at Sarah's slovenly habit like he used to, but it was no longer endearing. Instead, he tightened his fists and resisted the urge to toss the box and its contents into the yard.

He was about to lose everything if he didn't get his shit together. No matter how hard he tried, he ended up hurting her. No, he hadn't hit her, but his rage was at its peak, cocked and loaded, ready to mow down anything in its way.

Securing the cabinets, he headed into the house and hung his keys on their hook next to the fridge. He sank into a dinette chair and covered his eyes. Even here in the quiet his brain refused to give him peace. Vivid images from the past flashed - splattered, bloody bodies wrapped in white linen, tough, frozen-faced Marines faking bravado, fiery red rockets roaring over the FOB, and Yusuf's little hand reaching for candy. And now there was the more recent vision, Sarah's small form crouched in the hall, her shiny face full of tears. They didn't stop.

He jumped up. *Let's get this over with.* The chair crashed against the wall. He grabbed a beer and tossed it down before he reached the bedroom where he yanked open the closet door. He removed the shoe boxes off the top shelf until he found the leather holster containing his M9 Berretta. When was the last time he cleaned it? He grabbed the pistol and the cleaning kit and laid them on the bed. He sat on the bed, reached for the firearm, then froze. What was he doing? *You're not thinking about cleaning it.*

He leaped up as if the bed were a hot bed of coals. He paced, one end of the room to the other. Again and again. Each time he passed, he stared at the M9. First pass, he saw a villain, the devil. The next pass, he saw a friend. Like the M11 he carried in Iraq. That nine millimeter had gone everywhere with him. He had slept with it, ate with it... and killed with it.

Sweating profusely, he passed by again. His head throbbed. All other images vanished. He saw only ice blue steel. He resisted the iron pull to pick it up and downed another beer.

He escaped to the kitchen. Even there, his friend called. He couldn't leave it lying there. *What if Aiden got it? Aiden isn't here. Good thing.* He stomped back into the bedroom, this time bringing along the twelve pack. The second beer cooled the fire inside, so he uncapped another and sat down next to his steely friend. This unfeeling comrade had saved his life more times than he could count.

His gaze rested on the flowery chair in the corner and he thought of that day at the garage sale, now a lifetime ago, and of Sarah's delighted squeal at her discovery. Life had been so simple. On weekends he had tinkered with his 56 Merc which he'd been restoring since before he could drive. How many times had Sarah come out with sandwiches and lemonade and they ended up in the back seat making out? A hundred times and a hundred years ago. Their biggest worry had been making the rent and choosing which movie to watch on Saturday night. *Why can't it be like that again? But h*e knew why. He had seen too many things. He had done too many things. Things he would never talk about. Never.

Now the images were back, along with the fire in his gut. He grabbed the last beer. The room was dark. How long had he been sitting there? The empties sat in a row on the dresser. Another God-damned wasted day. Nothing changed. He wasn't going to change. Sarah deserved better. And Aiden. Sweet little Aiden. He couldn't even think of facing his son. Someday the boy would want to know about being a Marine, he already idolized his dad. What if Aiden found out what a coward his daddy was?

Alex wanted to cry. That disgusted him too. He was a Marine. Marines respect and protect their country and their family. When was the last time he had gone to see his mom? And the two buddies he had before he left, how were they? One studied computer engineering. Another had become a physical therapist. Both were married and had bought houses. They were living perfect lives. He was glad Sarah wanted him gone. He didn't want to be around anyone anyway.

He wrestled his duffle from the back of Sarah's closet but left his old clothes squashed in the back. Those were from a different life. He lugged the bag into the nursery, removed his cammies and sweats from that closet, folded them and placed them carefully in the bag.

Scanning the room he headed back to Sarah's room. Sarah's room. Was it already over? He was thinking it was. He shoved his extra boxers and socks from her dresser into the duffle, crammed his running shoes on top and zipped up the bag.

His eyes fell on the M9 still lying on the bed. He unzipped the bag, laid his protector gently next to his tennis shoes, and yanked the zipper closed. The grinding noise crept up his spine like a camel spider. He straightened, squared his shoulders, and headed to his truck, slowing in the kitchen long enough to grab the last twelve pack from the fridge.

He drove to Lake Perris State Park, paid the ranger at the kiosk for one night and found a campsite. Mid - week brought only a few, widely spaced campers. One motorhome, several spots down by the bathrooms, occupied the loop. The sign post in front of the rig spelled, "Camp Host." Its drawn curtains glowed in the damp, darkness creeping up from the lake. He finished off half of the twelve pack, hit the bathrooms and returned to his truck. Curling up on its bench seat, he drank until the alcohol blurred the images, slurred the voices in his head, and he slept.

Dawn's bright rays peeked over the hills and penetrated the windshield, forcing Alex's eyes open. He sat up, popped the top of a warm beer, and studied the movements of the camphost. An older man grasped a skillet on a camp stove and poked at sizzling bacon, the aroma seeped through the rolled up windows of Alex's truck. The man was thin but wore baggy sweats. Feathery white hair squeezed past the rim of an old cowboy hat and a long grey pony tail, waving to and fro in the morning breeze, dangled down his back.

The motorhome's door swung open and a hand poked out, holding plates and a bowl. The man smiled up at the figure inside and took the offerings. Alex watched, feeling invisible.

The thin man forked the bacon from the iron skillet onto one of the plates and dumped a bowl of beaten eggs into the pan. Alex's stomach growled, interrupting his trance. A more basic need pulled at his muddied mood. He had to pee. He shoved open the truck's door and set out on a fast pace, keeping his head down. He sprinted past the motor home toward the bathrooms.

"Hey! Semper Fi!"

Directly in front of the motorhome and the food's aroma, Alex jerked his head up, unable to ignore a fellow Marine. "Hey. Right back atcha."

Alex picked up his pace and escaped into the head. Releasing the night's payload of recycled beer, he zipped up, but dreaded going back outside. There was no way to avoid his cheery comrade. *Just move out.* He hunched down, and began his sprint back.

"Come join us, Jarhead." The man's deeply tanned face, marked by paler crow's feet that spread from his eyes made the old Marine's hair appear whiter. The aged warrior stood tall, giving a commanding appearance in spite of his slight build. Many pins, probably fishing lures, decorated his cowboy hat.

With his stomach's encouragement, Alex sucked it up, and veered over to the man. "Lance Corporal Alex Marsh, Sir."

The man pushed back his hat with a hand that lacked three fingers. "I saw your Corps sticker on your truck. I took it on myself to figure you needed to buddy up for breakfast." He extended his hand. "Lieutenant Colonel Robert Smith. Call me Monkey Man." He turned to the screen door. "Margie! Come on out and bring another plate. We have a guest."

Alex reached out to shake the man's offered hand. As they shook, the old Marine raised his left and wiggled the remaining two fingers on it. "Nam. I was a Tunnel Rat. How long you been out?"

"Iraq. I landed six months ago."

"It's rough when you first get back," the old man said. He scooped up the eggs from the skillet and laid them next to a couple slices of bacon on the plate, "Have a seat."

Margie threw open the motorhome door and bounced down the steps with plates and silverware in one hand, and a platter stacked with toast in the other.

"Will you bring out the honey and jelly, Robbie?" She said as she smiled up at Alex. "I'm Margie. I'm the one who keeps this Marine in line." She tilted her head up. Her eyes squinted in the warm sun and her gentle smile forced him to offer a weak grin in return as she sat down.

The Lt. Colonel came back out with a caddy of honey, butter and jelly. "Have a seat," the Marine repeated. "She's right you know. When I get squirrely, and I still do, she has a way of setting me straight."

Alex eased onto the bench across from Margie. Monkey Man sat down next to his wife, his long arm reaching around behind her small frame, and she leaned into him. He gave her a peck on the cheek.

"When she got tired of my crap and finally threw me out, I decided I'd better do something. She threatened to divorce me if I didn't get help. The thought of losing her scared me more than a million nights alone in the jungle. I ran to the nearest vet center for help." Again, the Colonel cradled his Margie. Alex flushed with jealousy knowing he and Sarah had lost what this couple had. He doubted they would ever have it again.

"I don't freak as often, but those nightmares of being in the tunnel still come back to haunt me, even after all these years. The scaredest I've ever been was on guard duty at night in Nam. That jungle was darker than dark. Some guys said they could smell the VC. I couldn't. But I'd hear sounds, movements. I knew they were out there. I fired off hundreds of rounds throughout the night. I just knew they were out there. God, I was scared. He soaked up the egg yolk with his toast and took a bite.

"In the morning a haze hung in the air and smelled of gun powder. Brass shell casings covered the ground. And there would be as many as fifty dead monkeys scattered on our perimeter." He laughed heartily. "That's why they called me Monkey Man.

"But seriously," he said, "War does something to you. Sometimes it's a moldy smell that takes me back. Rain and helicopters set me off. Don't ever think you'll be the same man you were before you left."

Alex stared at the old Marine. *How did he know?* It was as if the man had walked in his boots. Desperate to connect with someone who understood, he resisted the urge to hug the man, and yet the old man's words terrified him. If what Monkey Man said was true, he'd never get back to who he was. Alex turned to his breakfast, hunched over it, and choked it down like he was back in boot camp.

"Whoa there! There's more." Margie rose and came around behind him with the last of the eggs, scooping them onto his plate along with three more slices of bacon before he could protest.

"Sorry ma'am." But he continued shoveling in the food.

"Don't you worry, I love feeding young boys like you." She patted his back. "Don't you worry about anything." A tickly feeling in his gut startled him when she leaned down and lightly kissed the back of his neck. The touch of affection squeezed his throat shut. The last mouthful of food lodged half way down. He straightened up and laid down his fork.

"Margie misses mothering our boy. We lost him last year. He never came home from Afghanistan."

"I'm sorry Ma'am." Alex picked up his fork again and forced the last morsels of his meal past the boulder in his throat.

"We just want to thank you, Son, for your service. You need to know we are grateful. Monkey man and me, we're okay. We help each other." Margie fussed with the cleanup before she disappeared inside the motorhome.

Gathering a deep breath, Alex swung his leg over the picnic bench and stood up. "Sir, thank you for having me. Please, tell Margie thank you. I'm sorry for your loss. I really should be going."

The older man stood, his eyes pinched with pain. "It's not what you think. Our boy took his own life." The colonel stared into Alex's eyes then suddenly grabbed Alex in a hard embrace. His strength surprised Alex. When he released Alex, the old warrior stepped away and turned his back. As he did, Alex noticed a blue ribbon that stood out from the surrounding fishing lures on the old man's hat. Stunned Alex stared at the colonel's back. The man who called himself Monkey Man was the bearer of a Medal of Honor. When the old Marine turned around to face Alex again, Monkey Man ordered, "Keep your head down, son."

Alex sprang to attention, grabbed the man's hand and shook it vigorously. "I will Sir."

Long strides couldn't carry Alex away from the emotional scene fast enough. Back at his campsite he climbed into his truck, revved up the engine and threw it into gear. As his truck rolled past Medal of Honor winner, Lieutenant Colonel Robert Smith, the wounded warriors exchanged unofficial salutes to one another. Once out of sight, Alex stomped the accelerator, sprayed gravel, and sped away.

CHAPTER 10

Alex left the campground with no destination in mind. On auto pilot, he found himself in the parking lot of the Ponderosa Bar and Grill. He eyed his buddy's beat up old Dodge Ram parked on the back row and pulled up next to it. The paint wore a layer of dusty squiggle patterns from the dripping, damp mornings. A scattering of straw had spilled onto the asphalt from his open tailgate. Kevin lived off Scott Rd with his folks who raised and trained horses on their ten acre ranch.

Alex peered into the cab. Inside, several folders, thick with papers, lay on the bench seat while on the passenger floorboard rested a dog's water bowl. The truck bed held a fifty pound bag of dog food, a large puffy sheepskin cushion, and a bulging plastic bag from Pet Co, in it probably the rest of the requirements for owning a dog. It looked like Kevin got himself a service dog. But where was it?

Alex climbed out, lit a cigarette and sucked in long drags as he made his way to the door. He nodded to a couple of bikers leaning against their Harleys. They chugged beers and drew drags off their own rolled stogies. Alex pinched off the cherry on his smoke and slipped the butt into his vest pocket.

He pulled open the bar room's door. A strong odor of stale cigarettes, booze and mildew pushed past him, and escaped outside. The Ponderosa had been here as long as he could remember. The rancid smell of cigarettes had soaked into the dark wormwood paneling and would remain forever. He liked it. He'd been in shiny-clean bars. They were not for getting down, brawling-and-bawling-in-your- beer-drunk.

Allowing his eyes to adjust, he stood at the door and monitored the room. Too early for the noon crowd, the place was empty except the bartender and two dudes bookending the barmaid. The woman, who was a fixture, had been much younger when the bar first opened its doors years ago.

A light flashed from the back door and Alex tensed. A man, silhouetted by the daylight from outside, entered and approached the bar. The bar's colored lights illuminated the man's Clorox white shirt and Alex could read the uniform's emblem – Budweiser. Just the delivery guy. He jacked down his tension one notch.

Kevin sat alone at a table in a dim corner. He studied a brochure lit by his Mag light, his face shadowed by the flashlight like a boy scout at a campout, ready to tell ghost stories. So engrossed, he didn't notice Alex's approach. Alex flipped Kevin's cap and said, "Not good, buddy. Lack of diligence could get you killed." Kevin jumped as his attention flashed up at Alex. He smiled and said, "Hey,"

"You didn't have your eyes up and your head down." Alex grabbed a chair and attempted to pull it from the table, but its legs hung up on something under the table. He yanked harder until a large body of fur moved, and the chair pulled free.

The dog crawled out from under the table and sat in the aisle next to Kevin. "I see you got your dog. They let you bring it in here?"

Kevin stood, stepped back, and knelt down by the dog. "Meet Diego. I just got him. He is amazing. He wakes me at night when I'm having a nightmare. I've had him two weeks while they taught me all he can do, you know, the commands and all. " He wrapped his arm around the dog as it nuzzled his neck and thumped its tail on the peanut strewn floor. "Diego, greet."

The dog reached his foot up and pawed the air. Alex stared down as Kevin looked up and waited for his buddy to shake the dog's paw. Alex didn't bend down, but said, "Hey, Diego." *God, I don't even know how to act in front of a dog.*

Kevin stared up at his buddy. "What's wrong? You like dogs don't you?" The dog sat, staring expectantly at Alex. "I thought you said you used to have one?" Kevin rose from the floor and sat back down in his chair. Alex took a seat, avoiding the dog's stare. "You don't look so good, a little burnt around the edges."

"What's wrong with the dog? All he does is stare at me?" Alex twisted in his seat. "Tell the dog to lie back down."

Kevin motioned to Diego. "Under." The dog disappeared under the small table.

Alex checked out the bar again. Everyone acted normal. Except him. "Can I get a Coors over here?" His words came out short and loud. "And keep 'em coming."

The bartender glared at Alex, then focused on Kevin, who nodded letting the barkeep know to put the beer on his tab.

"The dog picks up on your tension." Kevin said. "It puts him on alert. So what's jerking your chain? You look like you've been out from under the wire too long."

"I spent the night at Lake Perris. Sarah and I split up. She wants some space, so I moved out." The barmaid slid a napkin on the table and slammed a bottle on it. Iced condensation slid down the neck and soaked the coaster. Alex grabbed the beer, the wet paper clinging to the bottom. His jaw clenched and imagined the bottle crashing against the wall.

Kevin took another drink. "Sorry, Alex."

"That's it! Sorry, Alex?" He glared at Kevin. His grip on the bottle made his knuckles ache. The old barmaid turned her head and Alex met her stare and growled, "What's your problem? " She brought her attention back to the barkeep and said something to her bookend friends. When they laughed amongst themselves Alex shoved his chair back and began to stand.

Kevin grabbed his forearm before it came off the table. "Chill." His friend's hard grip prevented his reaction to the bitch. "She's just having a drink with her friends, Alex."

Confused, Alex focused on his buddy's stare that now bore into him. Alex pressed his lips tight and nodded and said, "I'm good." Then he threw back the last swallow of beer, glanced toward the bar and hoped the barkeep was paying attention. The man rounded the corner with another and set it down. Alex slumped back into his chair.

"You gotta get a grip, man." Kevin said. "You gettin any help?"

"I'm okay. I got the paper work for the dog. Sarah's happy about that. I explained to her what the dogs do. She's skeptical but she's glad I have to do the counseling."

"Don't get your panties in a bunch, but that's what you need. I didn't think I needed it either, but it's helped."

"You? What did you need counseling for?" Kevin was like an older brother. "You're the toughest guy I know."

Kevin shrugged. "When do you start?"

"Tomorrow's my first group session, but I gotta find a place to stay."

"Tomorrow? I'm in that group. The guy that leads the group is solid. Hey, we'll be therapy buddies." Kevin's teasing smile wasn't returned. "Listen, why don't you stay in the old bunkhouse at the ranch? My folks have cut way back on their breeding and training and they laid off their stable boy when I came home from Iraq. They're down to five horses but I could use someone to help with the feeding since I'm working and going to school. They're going on a cruise next month so with my schedule..... Well, it would sure help out."

"Sure. Thanks. It'll only be temporary."

"That's okay buddy. Stay as long as you need. Follow me over and I'll get you set up." Kevin rose, threw some bills on the table and tipped his hat to the barkeep. He reached down and ruffled the dog's ears. "Come on Diego, let's go home."

Alex followed Kevin home, his rage drained, but the dregs of shame and guilt remained. That would never wash away.

CHAPTER 11

Alex tailed Kevin's truck up the long, dirt drive. The lane sliced between two pastures, green from the recent rains. Creamy snowcapped mountains stood at attention behind lush emerald hills. To his right grazed four sorrel horses, their noses buried in the heavy growth of grass, as their tails switched lazily back and forth. The pasture on his left held a black stallion, its coat gleamed a midnight blue, like the revolver in his duffle. The animal reminded him of a portrait of the Riderless Horse which had hung in his sergeant's office in boot camp. The proud steed raised his head, pointed his ears in Alex's direction and arched its neck. Like in the painting, his powerful haunches rippled in the sun. Winston Churchill's words popped into Alex's mind. *There is something about the outside of a horse that is good for the inside of a man.*

Alex pulled his focus back to the driving and slammed on the brakes in time to keep from rear ending Kevin's truck which had paused in front of a small cabin. Kevin's arm extended out the driver's window, pointing to the bunkhouse. He signaled to Alex and said, "Park there. Go on in. Make yourself at home. I'll let my folks know you're here."

Alex parked and turned off the ignition. He surveyed his new environment. As he climbed out and slammed his truck door, a black cat sleeping in a rocker on the porch sprang up and vanished around the side of the building. The empty rocker swayed back and forth in the breeze.

Now a Kenny Chesney melody about an old blue chair sang in his memory. *With the help of the winds....like an old trusted friend....nothing compares to the way that I see it [the world] when I sit in that old blue chair.* Get a grip, he told himself. He needed another beer. Alex hoisted his duffle from the truck bed and strode up on the porch. The screen door squeaked as he pulled it open and banged behind him when he stepped inside.

One room and bath, small but efficient, larger than his space at the FOB. No cement floors, walls, or ceiling, and no mortar rounds going off. He caught movement across the oak floor. A resident mouse scurried under the bed. *I guess the cat isn't a mouser.*

He slung his duffle on the bed, cracked open the door to a private bathroom, another luxury unheard of at the FOB. He was just beginning to feel he had arrived at the Ritz when the screech of a siren pierced the interior, loud and sharp enough to rattle the window. He dropped to the ground and fish tailed his body to follow the mouse beneath the bed.

With his senses on high alert, a small creak from the screen door canceled his push to follow the mouse. In one sweeping motion he rolled onto his back, rocked to his feet and grabbed for his weapon that wasn't there.

Kevin's silhouette filled the doorway. He held a stack of sheets, a blanket and pillows in his arms. "Whoa, buddy. It's only me. The siren's from the fire station behind our property." He walked to the window, pulled the gingham curtain back and gazed past the bars. "It's called progress. Remember when we used to be surrounded by ranches? One by one, they sold out. Now it's the fire station and a shopping center that backs up to our land. That's the reason for the bars."

Alex joined Kevin at the window. The iron bars were a plus. He ordered his muscles to relax, his pulse to quit pounding.

Kevin turned and laid the neatly folded stack of linens on the bed. "'Here you go, jarhead. I want to see a quarter bounce off that bed." Kevin punched his buddy's hard arm in a playful camaraderie. Alex's adrenaline-filled return punch carried a force one notch below combat mode.

"Yes Sir. Sargent, Sir!" Alex saluted and bowed to make light of the dramatic scene he had just played out. "Where's your dog?"

"I left him at the house to get acquainted with Mom and Dad. If they have anything to do with it they're going to make him the most spoiled service dog ever. I'll probably end up catering to the dog's every need instead of the other way around." Kevin faced Alex. "I'll leave you to get settled. Come on up to the house at six for dinner. Mom can't wait to feed you." He turned and was gone before Alex could decline.

It went with the place he figured. He'd have to be sociable. Anyway, he needed to find out what his duties were with the horses. He would not stay without paying his way.

He sorted through the linens to find scented soap nestled between the towels along with a travel shaving kit. Kevin's mom, Mrs. K, that's what he and Sarah and their friends had called her, was responsible for the special touch. After school, in another lifetime, he and his sister, Arlene, had come to ride the horses, a million summers ago.

He finished making the bed, hung up the towels, and checked his watch. Just enough time to shower and change. A small meow and the rattle of the screen door caught his attention. He looked through the mesh to find the cat banging the door with its paw. The cat peered up, and with a louder meow, demanded entrance. Alex pushed the door open and the creature rushed in as if it had been waiting for hours.

"What's your name?" The cat ignored the question, jumped onto the bed and rolled onto its back. "No answer? That's okay. I was top of my class in interrogations. I will torture it out of you." He moved to the bed, knelt down and scratched the cat's exposed belly. It stretched out even longer. It purred, loud like a smooth running Humvee. "Still no answer? I have my ways." He knelt down and stuck his face into the cat's furry belly, making a growling sound and laughed.

Suddenly he jerked his head up, as if he'd been shot, and stood quickly. What was he doing? Paralyzing guilt swept in and poisoned his warm feelings like a plague. A coldness swept over him as if he stared into the dead eyes of an insurgent, leaving no room for nicey nicies. The cat stared up at him, waiting. Its tail twitched. Alex locked eyes with the feline. His stomach lurched like a festering boil that had burst. It oozed with humiliation, frustration, and confusion. The twisted emotions continually drained, never giving him peace.

I can't even get along with a cat. The black ball of fur sprang down from the bed and rubbed against his pants leg. Back and forth. Back and forth. Alex avoided the feline's affections and stepped around it. He entered the bathroom and closed the door. He showered to the sound of a steady thump-thump-thump as the cat insistently batted at the bathroom door.

CHAPTER 12

Alex emerged from the shower shrouded in a cloud of steam. He never indulged under the hot massaging jets and dressed quickly. Always ready. But for the last six months, since he stepped off the big bird at Pendleton, he asked himself, *ready for what?* He inhaled the lavender scented soap Kevin's mom had tucked in with the towels. Yusuf's family had described the lavender fields which blanketed the Iraqi hills before the war. Alex recalled how the aunt's toothless smile transformed her tired, wrinkled face as she inhaled the memory of the aroma drifting through their village. Military tanks had long ago destroyed the fields, leaving only the smell of diesel and gun powder. Now, if anything smelled good in Iraq, it had arrived in a mail bag from the states.

Exiting the bathroom, Alex's heart slammed into his chest. He jumped and leaped over a dark, hairy form on the floor. The black ball of fur made no attempt to escape the wild antics of the warrior's dance, and instead, the animal squeaked out a tiny meow. Alex glared at the cat.

"I thought you were an IED." He stood, scrutinized the cat until he overcame his surprise, anger, and humiliation. Like a parade each emotional surge waved its flag, demanding his acknowledgement. As he stood in place, the feline jumped back onto the bed, flopped on its side, and again, exposed its tummy for rubbing.

Alex gathered up his control. "I guess you're a dud." Again, he asked, "What's your name?" And again, the cat ignored him, and began licking its paw. Alex laughed. "Since you won't identify yourself, I'll have to think up a name, maybe Spider, you're as big as a Camel Spider. He leaned in and scratched the cat's belly.

The loud purr reminded Alex of a coin operated vibrating hotel bed that he and Sarah had slept in. They had laughed at their purring voices until their tears soaked the pillows. He shrugged off the memory, grabbed his cap, and pushed open the screen door. Spider Cat slipped through his legs and sprinted outside, avoiding the slamming screen.

Kevin's mother craned her neck as she peered up at Alex. Smiling, she pushed open the front door and said, "Alex, please come in." She scanned him up and down. "You've grown into a fine young man." The wisp of a woman wore embroidered jeans and a denim jacket, her hair still in a page boy. Pleasant memories of his sister, Arlene, and him at the ranch pushed aside his nervousness. As kids, they had watched Mrs. K., more than once, handle a two thousand pound stallion twenty times her weight when the animal reared and stomped in rebellion. Mrs. K's magical 'horse-talk' had persuaded the stud to lower his head in submission and walk into his stall.

Alex reached out to shake Mrs. K's hand, but she dodged his impersonal offer, slipped her tiny frame past his stiff barrier, and wrapped her arms around his waist. "Come on in," she repeated. "It's so nice to see you all grown up, and a Marine, just like my Kevin." She released him, and her small hand took his elbow, steering him to the dining room. "Sit yourself down. Jerry's pulling the steaks off the grill now."

Alex shot Kevin, already seated, a pained expression. His friend smiled back clearly amused at his mother's clucking over his buddy.

The dinner hour ticked by as silverware tinkled and porcelain clinked in the background of polite conversation. No one questioned Alex's reason for being at dinner or his residency at the bunkhouse. Kevin's dog lay quietly under the table. After Mrs. K cleared away the dinner dishes, she slid a serving of lemon pie in front of him and said. "Made from the lemons off that tree by the bunkhouse. Do you remember how you and Arlene used to love those lemons? How is your sister and your mom? I haven't seen them since your homecoming party."

"Yes, ma'am, I do. I guess you got caught up on all the news at the party so you know Arlene's married. She's an RN and her husband's a veterinarian. They live in Oregon. Mom moved up there to be near them."

"Please tell them hello for me. I miss your mom. We used to enjoy shopping at the outlet stores."

Mr. K. devoured his pie and excused himself. He laid a big hand on Alex's shoulder and squeezed it. Alex didn't remember them being such 'touchy' people. "When you finish, Alex, come on out to the barn, I'll show you what needs to be done."

Alex forked up the last crumbs on his plate, excused himself and said, "Thank you. And ma'am, everything was very good." Kevin and Diego joined him and they headed outside for the barn. On the way Spider Cat appeared, shadowing Alex in the twilight. He knelt down and petted the cat. "You been waiting for me?"

"Looks like you have a friend," Kevin said.

They both peered down at the cat. "He reminds me of one of those Camel Spiders." Alex said. "You know, how they follow your shadow to stay in the shade when it's a hundred and thirty fucking degrees? Weird, huh? But cuter, don't you think?"

Kevin bent down and scratched the cat's ears. "When it was a kitten its mom got carried off by coyotes. Dad nursed it with a baby bottle until it could eat solid food. They texted pictures to me in Iraq of it curled up in Dad's hat. Nobody messes with Dad's hat." The cat rubbed against Kevin's hand, then made its way over to Diego, and began weaving between the canine's legs.

"Look at that. The dog doesn't even care."

"Diego's trained to be calm. He's still wearing his vest, but when I take it off, he's ready to play just like any other dog." He ran his hand over Diego's' back. "After you get done with Dad, come over to the pasture, we'll bullshit while I toss a tennis ball for Diego. He loves to play ball."

"Okay. I'll catch up with you." Alex stared at Kevin's back as he and Diego strolled away. Kevin was different since he got the dog. Relaxed? Maybe. Was he happy? His friend probably didn't carry all the shit in his head like he did.

Mr. K. showed Alex how to mix the mash for the old mare. "I feed at five in the evening and six in the morning. I appreciate you doing this for us, son. Kevin works late and goes to school so he doesn't have much time. Your help will be greatly appreciated. The misses and I don't get away much. We won't know how to act on our ten day cruise."

"No problem, Mr. K. I appreciate a place to crash." He paused. "It's just temporary."

"Stay as long as you need."

Alex and Mr. K. finished their chores. The barn's musky interior filled with the crunching sounds of the feeding horses. The oldest mare, Miss Belle, hung her head over her stall door, her eyes half closed. Alex moved over to her and bent closer. He rubbed his cheek against her velvet muzzle.

Mr. K. hung back in the shadows. "She's off her feed again. She's old and tired. Keep an eye on her. I'll have the vet out, again, when we get back."

Spider Cat was nowhere to be seen when Alex trekked over to the pasture. The sunset lacked the splendor for which California was famous, and Alex felt cheated. Maybe Mother Nature knew he didn't deserve the spectacle. He sat down next to his comrade and watched Kevin throw a ball and Diego race to retrieve it. Their seat, a tree trunk that had served its fallen years as a bench, had also been the step-up for them, as children, to mount old Belle during their riding classes.

Puffing and out of breath, Diego plopped down in front of Kevin, but didn't drop the ball. He chewed the rubbery orb like a piece of tough meat, too big to swallow. He panted, and air rushed in and out, around the saliva soaked ball. He chomped and gasped but didn't drop his prize. Instead, he rose from his spot, walked over to a bucket of water and released his possession into the water to float while he lapped. Sated, he snapped up the orb by dunking his head beneath the surface. When he pulled his head from the pail with the ball between his teeth, water flooded from his mouth. He plodded back to Kevin's side, sank to the ground with an umph and carefully placed the toy between his paws.

The comrades sat in silence, watching the dog until the shadows lengthened. When the cover of darkness hid all but the night sounds, Kevin asked, "So it's not going too good?"

"What do you think? It's going just peachy. I can't sleep. I scare my wife and kid and I want to sign up again. Yeah, it's going just peachy keen." Alex stood up, edgy and unable to trust the area was clear without night vision scopes, and angry at Kevin for asking. "I'm gonna hit the rack. It's been a long day."

Kevin glanced up. "I'll see you tomorrow at the counseling appointment."

"I'll be there." Alex held himself in check and resisted the habit to hunch down and sprint back to the bunkhouse. When the screen door banged shut behind him, he slumped, relieved to be alone. His gaze fell to Spider Cat who lay curled up on the bed. "Shit."

CHAPTER 13

Spider Cat slowly uncurled and arched his back in a long stretch as if time belonged to him. The cat's attitude pissed Alex off. He threw his hat onto the small desk and glared at the animal. The cat returned his stare, then turned its back and twitched its tail.

Alex stepped closer. "What do you want?" His words signaled the cat to jump down and rub against his leg. He restrained the urge to kick it. Everyone had to get close, Kevin, Sarah, even the cat. His skin crawled at the thought. Aggravation pounded against his temples. What was wrong with him?

He sank onto the bed and buried his face in his hands that smelled like horses. He was losing everything important, everything he had worked so hard for. He had not signed up for this roller coaster ride. The situation terrified him more than any occupied haji village, and worse than a hundred rounds of ammo hammering against his Humvee. Where had he gotten the illusion he was home safe? Bullshit. He would never feel safe again. I don't want to feel safe. Can't let my guard down. No one understood. The joy of kissing his wife or hugging his son had been wiped out as thoroughly as if an IED had done the job, any tenderness was replaced by rushes of guilt and shame. Images, memories, and nightmares continued to flare up unexpected, like insurgents. He commanded, he screamed, he even begged his mind to stop. Nothing worked.

He wanted to go back. He yearned for the rush. He wanted the pride of being a Marine again. His comrades needed him. He had abandoned them. He enjoyed the killing. What about just one more tour? What was he admitting? No, he couldn't want all that. He couldn't hurt Sarah anymore. He'd promised. Sarah would leave, and he would lose his son. But he couldn't keep his word. Who was he kidding? He couldn't go on. His heel touched the duffle he had shoved under the bed. He should unpack. He grunted. Temporary my ass. He was never going home.

He reached down, pushed Spider Cat away. Leaden arms made him weak and the bag too heavy to lift. He left it on the floor and slid the duffle out in front of him. Numb fingers unzipped the bag and pulled out a stack of underclothes. Legs that felt like stumps refused to let him stand. His ribs squeezed air from his lungs as if his chest were wrapped in Kevlar and duct taped, ready for a mission, ready to lug full combat gear up a soft hot, hundred-and-fifty-fucking-degree sand dune that burned the soles of his boots. Hell must be like that. How could he want to go back? He couldn't go back.

Too tired to rise, he laid the stack of briefs on the bed. Reaching in for more clothes, his hand touched his weapon. His fingers, once numb, now tingled from the coolness of the iron as his piece invited them to curl around its grip. A lightness like a slow, floating drug slid through his veins.

He held up the gun and studied its steel lines as if seeing it for the first time. Even in the darkness it shined - the metal, blue and smooth. He rested the muzzle against his cheek.

The scent of a firefight and rotting bodies strewn across sifting dunes carried him away. He stood over the insurgent, his persuader digging into the man's temple. In the darkness, his finger twitched as he imagined the power and control - and pride - when he pulled the trigger. One less dirty, double crossing, fucking haji. One more for the team.

The image of the haji's face, frozen with terror, filled his vision. He was a Marine. No fear! The heaviness that had weighed him down evaporated. He sat at attention. Power, control, and pride flooded through him.

Alex's elbow jerked as Spider Cat bumped it. The pistol's icy muzzle pushed against his hot skin and he came back to the room. He opened his eyes to the reflection in the dresser mirror. A jarhead, a gun to his head, stared blankly back at him. There was no haji - the reflection was no stranger.

He stared at the likeness of Lance Corporal Alex March, USMC as if he were someone else. The cat nudged his elbow again, and he saw the reflection of his persuader press harder against his temple. The power, control, and pride he thrived on in Iraq were nowhere to be found in the mirror. Those feelings had not gotten off the bird with him. They were gone. Unless he went back. He should do the right thing. He should end this now. He recited the Marine's Prayer.

"Almighty Father, whose command is over all and whose love never fails, make me aware of Thy presence and obedient to Thy will. Keep me true to my best self, guarding me against dishonesty in purpose and deed and helping me to live so that I can face my fellow Marines, my loved ones, and Thee without shame or fear. Protect my family. …"

Protect my family.

What was he doing? Did he want to do this? Would this protect his family? Another image of a nameless, fellow Marine flashed into his mind.

The Marine lay on a gurney as Alex helped the medics load the wounded warrior into the chopper. Half of the Marine's face and skull lay mixed in a sand dune like a rice medley. Still, the warrior had said, "Tell my wife I love her. Promise me." Alex had only nodded because his throat swelled shut to keep the bile in his belly. He heard the warrior had survived.

The clearness of the memory shot down his brilliant suicide mission – a plan as sweet and as alluring as a temptress – a solution that would end his misery. It was one thing to survive an IED, but to survive a suicide? He couldn't take the chance. He watched the jarhead in the mirror lower his arm and shove the weapon back into the bag. Alex turned away, unable to look into the man's defeated eyes. Sarah deserved a husband, and Aiden a father. Yet, if he stayed he didn't know how to stop the destruction he caused.

He rolled back onto the mattress and stared at the knots in the log ceiling. The long night passed like all the others – more bloodied bodies, countless heart wrenching memories of comrades dying in his arms, and too many children who didn't play. When sleep came, the nightmares woke him, reminding him to stay alert.

He wouldn't live, but he'd stay alive.

Morning found him fully dressed, in a fetal position with Spider Cat nestled by his neck. His fingers brushed lightly across the purring form. He turned his head toward the animal's warmth and smelled its fur. The memories of unending, cold desert nights, and the hot smells from the baking Iraqi sun dissipated, replaced by a quiet calmness that emanated from Spider Cat. The warrior had made it through another night.

CHAPTER 14

Spider Cat marched behind Alex as he made his way to the barn. Low morning clouds hugged the hills, unable to climb up the mountains. Their cotton veil wrapped around the entire range that circled the valley. Alex compared the dawn to an Iraqi morning. No minarets called for prayer. There was no need. The American landscape performed the spiritual service.

Alex prayed for peace, not for the Far East, but for his tortured soul.

Last night terrified him. He had come close to finding peace, but only for himself. He couldn't go AWOL from his family, but he was aware he was lost outside the wire and only a higher power, be it Buddha, Allah, God, whoever, could lead him home. He faced the sunrise. It warmed his face but didn't reach the coldness inside. Spider Cat rubbed up against his leg, sat, and stared up at him, waiting.

"Okay Spider. Let's get er done." He yanked open the barn doors and morning burst into the dank interior.

Reaching into the feed sack, he scooped a coffee can full of grain, and dumped the contents into a bucket. The old mare snorted and shuffled in her stall. He opened her door and she sniffed the contents in the pail he held under her nose.

"Come on girl. You gotta eat. Keep your strength up. You can't give up yet." He poured the grain into her feed bucket. She buried her muzzle in it, her velvet lip quivered, and she nibbled tentatively. "That a girl. All the boys and girls you used to give lessons to would be heartbroken if you quit now." He slid his hand under her silken mane. It draped over the arch of her still proud, muscular neck. She began to eat while he scratched her forehead. He studied her big eyes, shrouded with lids too tired to open all the way, the powerful crunching sound of her jaws soothed him.

He was tired too, exhausted, and unable to sleep more than a couple of hours at a time. Sleep was peppered with green, night vision images and grating sounds, rat a tats and explosions, foreign chatter, and killing chants. There was no peace. Since he hit the tarmac, forgotten memories and nightmares repeatedly flashed into his mind with the power and frequency of firebombs. They exploded with no apparent rhyme or reason and could only be confronted with guilt, shame and doubts of what he'd done and what he should have done.

The mare licked the bucket clean. He laid his cheek on her soft velvety nose and smelled her horsey odor. She snickered in response. Setting the pail down, he slid his hands over her body still hard and sleek. Her graceful lines caught the dim light, swept up and danced around as if to the music of a soundless sympathy. He continued to caress the horse, absorbing her quiet energy. A tranquility seeped in, warming him deeper than the sun had done. *When was the last time he had paused his life, like this?*

He finished feeding the others. While they crunched, he mucked the stalls and replenished their water. He was sweeping up traces of hay strewn across the aisle when his cell vibrated against his leg. Digging the device from his pocket, electricity shot into his hand when Sarah's face lit up the screen. His fingers trembled and his throat slammed shut. The woman could bring him to his knees. With a look.

"Hey." His ears rang and his stomach churned.

"Hi." Her voice sang an octave higher.

He squeezed the phone. "Are you and Aiden okay?"

"Yes. Yes. I was worried about you. Are you okay? Where are you staying?"

"I'm at Kevin's. I'm trying to give you some space."

"Oh, well. I called ....I just called to let you know we're back home now. I thought maybe you'd like to come over this afternoon, after Aiden wakes up from his nap? Maybe we could take him to the park?

Her voice sounded far away. He sank onto a bale of hay in front of the mare's stall. "Sure."

He felt his cap lift off his head and he twisted around. The old mare, with his cap between her teeth, tossed her head up and down, waving it like a flag. He heard the air rushing from his lungs. He was laughing.

"Alex?"

"Oh sorry, honey." While pressing the phone to his ear, he grabbed his cap and engaged in a tug of war with the horse. "I can't wait to see you and Aiden. I'll come about three?"

"Great. We'll see you then."

He shoved the phone into his pocket as the horse released her grip on his cap. Unable to catch his balance, he stumbled backwards, over the feed bucket, and landed on his ass in the middle of the aisle. Spider Cat appeared, and jumped on his lap while the mare tossed her head, raised her lip and whinnied.

Alex's hands cupped Spider Cat's head, looked him in the eye, and said, "Big ass Marine found beaten up by an old horse and a cat." He remained on the floor, laughing and petting the cat. "But he gets to see his family." He set the purring feline on the ground and stood with a lightness he hadn't felt in a long time. He hung up the broom and the bucket on their respective pegs and headed back to the bunkhouse. He had to get through the counseling appointment first, but he felt good. He would ace the appointment.

He eased his truck down the long drive and merged into the moving traffic. He rolled down his window and breathed in the invigorating, chilly morning. Changing lanes, he approached an intersection, and came to a stop at a red light before turning right. An SUV sped up behind him, so close it almost rear ended him. The light changed and the driver leaned on his horn.

"Come on out, you son of a bitch!" Alex found himself at the SUV's driver door, pounding his fists against the SUV's dark tinted window. He yanked on the Escalade's handle and kicked the door panel.

"Hey, Marine. Stand down."

The command penetrated his rage. He stopped and swung around. A civilian in slacks, pale blue dress shirt and black tie stood behind him. The hatless stranger's dark hair was cut tight, roan colored, like the old mare's. The Marine's confusion must have flashed across his face.

"At ease, Marine. You're home now."

The SUV's door swung open and the driver jumped out. "What's the matter with you? You must be crazy! The cops are on their way." The SUV man turned to the civilian bystander. "Did you see what he did? I thought he was gonna kill me!"

"It's all right now." The observer looked at the Escalade. "There's no damage. Why don't you let it go? Here's my card. If there's any problem I'll take care of it."

The driver glanced at the card. A gold embossed government seal lit up in the sun. He dropped his attitude. "Sure. Okay."

The Escalade disappeared before Alex could evaluate what had happened. He recalled the vehicle on his ass, the horn blaring, and being ordered to stand down.

"You're okay, Marine. Why don't you move on?" The man ushered him to his truck, the door still open, Alex climbed in.

"Thank you, Sir." Alex reached over and shook the man's hand.

The nameless stranger shut the driver's door and handed him his business card. "Carry on."

The mysterious man disappeared in his rear-view mirror. *What the hell happened?* Alex shrugged, shoving the incident in to join the many others - into the already crowded compartment in his brain.

CHAPTER 15

Once again Alex pried his white knuckled fingers from the wheel. Rubbery legs threatened to give way when he stepped out of his truck at the veteran's center. He hung onto the door and lit a cigarette. Sucking in the nicotine, he resisted the urge to grab a warm beer from the tool chest in the truck bed. They probably drug test you. He took another deep drag, pinched the butt, and shoved it in his pocket. Slamming the door, he headed for the entrance.

"Hey!" Kevin waved from his parking space and approached with a grin. His dog kept pace beside him. "You made it. You ready for this?"

Kevin slapped him on the back and Alex grunted. They walked the rest of the way in silence.

Inside Kevin took the lead. "This way." They joined others heading down a hall and entered a room with a circle of chairs in the center. A man dressed in slacks and pale blue shirt, his back facing them, talked to a group of men and a couple of women. Several in the huddle murmured easily to one another and held leashes as their dogs sat patiently beside them.

As they approached, the man in the blue shirt turned and said, "Hey Kevin!"

Alex paused. The man's eyes shifted to Alex in recognition. He was the stranger who had defused the situation on the street twenty minutes ago. *Aw shit, he must be the counselor.* Alex and the stranger exchanged a slight nod, and the man turned back to his conversation, allowing Alex his dignity. *Great.* The psych was going to call him out for sure. Well, he had a reason to let loose on the Escalade. You don't threaten someone without retaliation. Jesus!

Alex stuck close to Kevin until his buddy abandoned him to talk to a couple already seated. He glanced around the room, shifting from one foot to the other.

"Okay folks, let's get started." The psych took a seat, clipboard in hand, as he and the others scattered to their seats.

Alex picked a spot as far from the blue shirt as possible but, no matter where he sat, he was in his direct line of vision. "I'm Foster. Welcome." The voice came from a vet seated beside him.

Alex glanced down and shook the hand offered. "Lance Corporal Alex March." Alex's mouth watered for the beers in his toolbox.

"Hello everyone. For the new people, let me introduce myself. I'm Mark Parrish. We'll start off with introductions and then spend the first hour sharing." *The first hour! Christ!* "Then we'll take a break. During the second hour I'll try to shed some light on why you're having so many difficulties. Any questions?"

The sharing rolled around the circle like a roulette ball, many passed until it stopped at a female vet seated next to Mark. The thin, buff woman, her face drawn with tension wore a t-shirt and shorts. As she spoke, she rocked to and fro. She'd been a medic and complained she couldn't sleep. Drawn in by her story, Alex, elbows to his knees, leaned forward. She told the group she had been haunted by the image of a young Marine who had lost his legs from an IED. She'd been unable to save him. Her dreams, she said, were crowded with the images of comrades whom she had loaded onto the chopper and sent off, never knowing if they survived or not. Guilt consumed her. "I treated the injured like carcasses in a meat packing plant. Suck it up and press on. We all said that." She buried her face in her hands. Her husband, who had done two tours, had his own issues. "We both come down too hard on the kids."

An airman, who seemed underage, told his story next, his rosy cheeks smooth with youth. He had been stationed on a carrier. One of his duties was to clean the deck of oil and fuel spills from the aircraft. In the middle of the night he got called out to what he assumed was a routine spill.

"Not so," he said. "An airman on deck had been sucked into one of the jet engines. The turbos had spat out the poor soul like red sawdust from my dad's wood chipper. Small red chunks covered the deck." The kid hung his head. The group's silence amplified the boy's deep breathing. "But I did my job. Every time I see the smallest piece of trash lying on the ground I think of that night."

The stories labored on. One Marine twisted his hands in knots while he shared. He and his wife had separated because he couldn't control his rage, the last argument, over a screw driver she had left lying on the tool bench. Alex thought of the morning's incident with the SUV.

Kevin's turn to share came and his buddy related his own combat experiences, many Alex had already heard. He also described his difficulty in coping when he had returned home. Alex, who had still been deployed, was unaware Kevin had suffered the similar problems. "Until I got Diego," Kevin said, and his eyes glassed over with tears. Alex flushed in embarrassment for him.

"This dog has changed my life." Kevin petted Diego, who in response, sat up and laid his head on Kevin's lap. "Every time I stress in a crowd, or I think I'm losing it, I look down at him. I trust him. If he's calm, I can bring it down. He's my team mate. I know Diego has my back." Alex shifted and squirmed in his chair. Alex had never seen a Marine cry. Never.

Too soon, the ball stopped at Alex. The veterans' chronicles had brought back too much. His gut churned. He stared at the ground. His ears rang and he felt the sensation of floating. Could this be how gangrene infested bodies felt as they rotted along the roadside? In his mind an image appeared of a white gossamer robe splattered with blood, fluttered like the sail on a ghost ship appeared. He smelled the death and hoped the group didn't notice him shiver. Caught up in the séance, Alex began to relate his own demons.

"Lieutenant Reikert and I squatted on a rooftop. I had borrowed his Tabasco to rub in my eyes to stay awake. The sun was reaching over the ridge and it lit up our patrol area. You could hear the minarets as they spread the muezzin's chant into the cool air. I remember thinking how the sing song voice was an attempt to disguise the destruction that hung over the land, like the black veils the women wore. To us, it was the signal for the coming day's violence to begin. Reikert shoved the Tabasco bottle back into his jacket and pushed up to peer over the wall.

"When Reikert's helmet cleared the barrier's protection, his face inside exploded." Alex looked around the circle. "Like Gallagher's watermelon. Remember that 70's entertainer who took a sledge hammer to a melon? It was like that. I froze, I didn't even flinch. As if nothing happened. I stayed crouched on that slippery roof, carpeted in shell casings, and clutched my M-16. I began shaking and couldn't stop."

Alex's knee jerked and his heel tapped a fevered cadence. He stared into the past and felt his words bleeding out from some deep place inside.

"It was dark before the commander came looking for us. I was still there, in the same position. Reikert's helmet had rolled to the other side of the roof."

Alex ran his hand over his head, covered his eyes, but refused to cry. Relating his cowardice filled him with shame, and worse. He had forgotten the entire incident, and Reikert. How could he have forgotten? What kind of man would not remember?

A hand touched his knee. He wished Foster would leave him alone. He didn't want the man's sympathy. Surprised he felt anything, he glanced down. It wasn't Foster. The hand was a paw. Diego's paw. The animal's touch brought the wounded warrior back to the room. Diego's black eyes looked up at him. Unable to turn away from them, their umber pools drew Alex into their depths and his heart swelled inside his chest. He surrendered to their magic and in desperation he grasped the offer of Diego's love and acceptance. He engulfed the dog in his arms.

The room was still, like before first light, before the minarets rang out. Alex straightened, released the dog and looked around. He met Kevin's gaze. "I see what you mean." The group came alive and clapped. Feeding off the group's energy, Diego jumped up and placed a big kiss on his face and then bounded back to Kevin.

CHAPTER 16

"With that let's take our break." Scraping chair legs, back slapping, and conversation filled the room. Alex approached Kevin and Diego, squatted down and massaged the dog's ears. "Hey boy, thanks for what you did. You're a good dog." Diego again laid his paw on Alex's knee, nuzzled his arm, and licked his face.

Kevin pulled his dog back. "He's not supposed to lick you on the face."

Alex laughed. "He can do whatever he wants. If you knew where I was last night...well, you're right, he's a miracle dog." Again, he hugged the dog, who reacted by jumping up and barking.

"He needs to go outside. Let's grab some java," Kevin said.

In the courtyard, the two Marines drank coffee and talked to the other vets milling around. Kevin turned to Alex. "Diego goes to the bathroom on command. Can you believe that? Watch." Kevin reached down and unsnapped the leash. "Do your business, Diego." The dog wandered a few paces away, peed, then returned and sat at attention in front of Kevin.

"That's incredible."

"A lot of training goes into these dogs." Kevin snapped the leash on Diego's collar.

"Do you remember Sarah's friend, Judy who has the grooming salon?" Alex said. "She trains dogs. Sarah told me Judy took a leave of absence from her business to start a service dog program in Illinois called K-9s For Warriors."

"Diego was trained in the women's prison here in Chino by a woman doing twenty years for armed robbery."

A bell rang and they followed the others back inside.

Mark waited for everyone to settle. "I'm here to help you understand what you are going through. I am going to try to break it down for you. First, you've all been trained for combat. Combat training teaches you to react. In the heat of a fire fight, there is no time to think. If you stop to think, you're dead. The fact that you're here and made it back proves you were good at your jobs.

"Second, even if you hadn't been trained, your brain trains you. Anytime anyone experiences a traumatic situation, when their life is threatened, the brain remembers every detail, even if the person doesn't. Every detail is stored for quick access, like an app on your phone. Your brain's primary function is survival, to keep you safe.

"For an example, you're walking down the street and a mangy dog jumps out from behind an aromatic bush, maybe it's a lavender bush, and bites you on the leg. The next time you walk down the same street your brain will remember that place, that bush, and the smell of lavender – triggers, if you will - and your heartbeat will automatically race in anticipation of an attack. The brain will not have to clear the details with command. Instead, it clicks on the app – instant reaction.

"Now let's assume the dog's attack was so traumatic you don't remember it happening. This happens a lot in car crashes. The brain becomes overloaded because you can only handle so much trauma, so your mind pushes the event into the unconscious. So now, you walk down the street, you smell lavender, and begin to panic. You think you're crazy because you don't remember the initial incident, but your brain does, and don't forget, its function is to keep you safe.

"But let's say you're in your neighbor's yard and the same bush grows near his patio. His dog, which you've known from a pup and has played with his kids and yours, comes up to greet you. Your brain remembers the bush's smell, the size of the dog and the fast movement toward you. Your brain clicks on the app, ready to save your life. Your heart races and you immediately react. You, as well as your neighbor, think you're losing your mind by reacting to a dog you've known for years.

"Now take the mangy dog incident to Iraq, jack the event up to occur 24-7 for a year and what do you have? A brain keyed for survival mode tuned into so many triggers you can't even count them. You're a reactor, a reacting machine with no kill switch installed."

Mark leaned back in his chair. All eyes stared at him. Some heads nodded, others tilted in doubt.

"So the reactions you experience over and over that you think are unreasonable are only the brain's attempt to keep you alive – and to keep you safe from experiencing the emotional and physical traumas it remembers.

Alex understood what Mark was talking about. The SUV had reminded him of a cargo truck, honking, and barreling toward him one day on patrol. He and Eddie yelled, ordering the vehicle to stop and when it didn't, the gunner took it out, killing the driver and its passenger. When they inspected the truck, the only cargo was fruit from the market.

The Marine sitting across from him spoke again. "I just realized I went into a rage over the screwdriver because, being in the mechanics pool, tools had to be put away, if even one was lost when we were in route, it could mean life or death. Our lives depended on how fast I could get the hummer rolling again. We were sitting ducks 'til I got the piece of shit running again. A lost screwdriver can mean life or death."

The medic chimed in, "Every time I hear a chopper I get emotional. I want to cry, scream, and hit someone, all at the same time."

"Good work everyone," The therapist said. "Start recognizing your triggers. You may not be able to stop your reactions, but explain them to your loved ones. They will be more supportive if they understand. See you all next week."

Alex approached Mark as the others exited the room and offered his hand. Thank you sir."

"Glad you came, Marine. Hope it helped."

"Yes Sir. It did, Sir. Yes, Sir." He continued pumping the man's arm. "Thank you Sir." Embarrassed by his own gushing, Alex released the man's hand, turned and left.

Before the Veteran Center's door swung shut behind him, he had lit a cigarette and sucked in deep drags as he crossed the parking lot. Dizzy from the nicotine, he reached into the tool box and grabbed two warm beers. Climbing into the cab, he popped the top on first one, tossed it back, did the same to the second, and then picked up the card on the seat from the morning's incident. Mark Parrish, United States Department of Veterans Affairs. Small world. He would probably be in jail if it hadn't been for Mark Parrish, U.S. Department of Veterans Affairs.

CHAPTER 17

Alex revved up the truck's engine. He slammed it in gear and burned rubber on the asphalt. The surge of horsepower did not stir up the rush it had as a teen. As a Marine, he required bigger, real, life-threatening events to release the amount of adrenaline which he was now addicted.

He was off to see his family. They were going to the park so he swung into the 7-11's parking lot. Inside, he picked up sandwiches and potato salad. As an afterthought, he purchased a small blanket, chips, and a stuffed toy for Aiden. One six pack of soda and two of Coors topped off his inventory for an afternoon in the park.

He couldn't wait to tell Sarah about his experience with Diego. When Alex entered the house, Aiden squealed in delight at the sight of his daddy. Dressed in small khaki shorts, a cammie T-shirt and little boots, the boy reached up to his dad and Alex lifted him into his arms.

Sarah waited with a warm smile as she enjoyed the reunion of her son and his father. She pushed a cap with the Marine emblem onto Aiden's head and said," There you go tough guy." Then she turned to Alex. "Come on in the kitchen. Let me get my jacket. And I made cookies. Snicker doodles, your favorite."

"Great. Thanks, Honey. I've got everything else in the truck." On the drive to the park Sarah seemed her old self as she talked about her job, recounting the latest events in her customers' lives.

They arrived at the park, and Alex grabbed the bags while Sarah carried Aiden and she led them to a spot near the play area.

"This is perfect." Sarah began to spread the blanket on the grass.

"Not here." The spot had no bushes or trees, too open. "Over there." Alex motioned to a grassy place tucked in the corner of the park, sheltered by shrubbery, yet offered a clear view of the surrounding area. Sarah shrugged after making sure she could still monitor the playground.

They spread out the blanket and Sarah propped Aiden against her as she sat down. Walking the sandy area of the playground, Alex policed every square foot for any dangerous or unusual objects. A soda can hidden under the see-saw sent his pulse racing. He tried to will his body to relax but couldn't. He scanned the rest of the park, wishing he had his revolver, just in case. *Calm down*. When he returned from his surveillance, Sarah sensed his mood. "Relax," she said and touched his arm.

He jerked away. She turned, shaking her head. She left him alone and concentrated on Aiden. The boy babbled in delight as he crawled around in the grassy area. Sarah laughed as their little monkey covered a great distance in a small amount of time. Alex steeled himself from reacting.

"We can still see him from here." Sarah said, coaxing Alex to retreat to the blanket. She sat down and pulled his hand to join her. He conducted one more sweep of the bushes and then sat down.

"I called the vet center yesterday," she said. "They told me they're offering a Seminar and Sharing Session for spouses and the family members of the veterans. I signed up for it. Mom convinced me that I should try harder to get along with you." She smiled up at Alex and leaned against him. "She said getting along with Dad when he got home from Nam was like trying to calm a cat in a room full of rockers. She said they separated a couple of times."

"Really? Your folks?"

"I was shocked too. When mom told me what he was like and some of the things he still does, like having nightmares, he's just like you."

"Maybe your dad should come to the group therapy with me. It was amazing, Sarah. And the psych is cool….for a civilian." Alex recounted his morning encounter with the SUV and his interaction with Diego. "I'm telling you, Honey, it was like the dog talked to me and said, 'It's okay, Marine. You're good." He took Sarah's hands and pancaked them between his. Her small palms nestled on his as he absently fingered her wedding ring. "When that dog laid his paw on my leg and stared into my eyes, I felt all weird inside, I can't explain it."

Sarah leaned her back against his chest. Alex heart pounded, but this time, not because he was walking point. He brushed a strand of hair from her brow.

She twisted around, and gazing into his eyes she said, "That's nice, Alex. I mean about the dog, but what I'm trying to say is, I'm willing to work at this. I don't want to lose you, though lately I feel that I already have. Like you left the part of you that I love in Iraq."

"We'll get through this," he said, and wrapped her tight in his arms. He tilted her chin up to kiss her. When her lips parted, and she returned his caress with passion, hope surged through him. The tenderness long overdue.

When they pulled away, she leaned back against his chest just as she caught sight of Aiden. Her laughter vibrated against Alex's chest and she said, "Look at Aiden." His son sat near the sandy edge of the playground. A mother with her toddler, who was dressed in pink ruffles, sat beside Aiden. The babies waved their arms at one another and babbled in conversation.

"The girls are chasing him already." Alex said. Pride washed away his earlier, basic sensations. These two people in his life made him long to be the man he wanted to be. Living without Sarah and Aiden, or hurting them was not an option.

Alex snatched up the stuffed giraffe he'd purchased and stood. "I'd better create a distraction before our son develops a more complicated interest."

The day rushed by as the proud parents watched their son giggle and carry on with his new toddler girlfriend. A late afternoon chill forced them to pack up their belongings. Alex rose, then reached down to help Sarah up. She sprang up with little assistance and kissed him again. His body's reaction below the belt embarrassed him as if he were a teen. "We'd better head back."

Sarah gathered their blanket and Alex scooped up their protesting toddler, who gyrated in an attempt to be put down.

"When he's tired he gets cranky." Sarah said, and grabbed the boy's cap before it fell off.

When Alex strapped Aiden in his car seat, the boy fell asleep before they were a block from the park. An electric quiet filled the truck's cab on the ride home. Alex knew what he was thinking, and wondered if Sarah thought the same. The excitement of the possibility kept him aroused.

He carried Aiden to his room and laid him in his bed. Gently he removed one of the little black boots when his mind took a sharp turn.

Yusuf stood before him. The boy's smile spread across his face and he reached out for candy. Alex released his son's pudgy leg as if the limb had burnt his hand. He rushed to the bathroom, dropping to his knees, and retched into the latrine. Sweat beaded his forehead, his t-shirt clung to his clammy skin, and he grasped the toilet seat to contain the dizziness.

Spent, he hung his head over the bowl. Hearing Sarah rustle around in the kitchen, he said a silent prayer, thankful she hadn't seen. He grabbed a towel, dampened it, and wiped away the nausea. His composure regained, he returned to the sleeping baby and finished undressing him.

His electric mood extinguished, he paused at the kitchen door and leaned his bulk against the frame. Sarah, her back to him, slipped the left over cookies into a baggie.

"I'll be going," he said to her back. "We don't want to rush things."

She didn't look up. She set the cookies aside, straightened, and wiped down the counter. "No, I guess not." She continued wiping. "Mom and Dad are handling Aiden's birthday invitations. You are coming? They've invited your mom and sister, too."

He came up behind her, pulled her hair aside, and kissed the back of her neck. "I wouldn't miss my son's first birthday party for anything."

She leaned against his chest. He gently turned her around and cupped her face in his hands, hands that had killed so many. Anger pushed the thought back, and he kissed her hard. She pressed against him and his brain exploded. Electric jolts made every muscle react with anticipation. He gathered her in his arms and covered the distance to the bedroom in seconds. When she pulled his head down to meet her lips, he melted into the powerlessness of surrender and cried out like an injured animal from the passion.

Spent and satisfied, tangled in bed sheets, they stared at the ceiling. Alex spoke first. "We don't want to rush things."

"No we don't."

CHAPTER 18

Sarah's eyes, soft with spent passion, fluttered and focused on Alex. He sank into hers and said, "I don't want to hurt you anymore. I can't control myself sometimes."

The tip of her tongue traced the soft lines of her lips that curved at the corners. Her green eyes were liquid emeralds. His body stirred again.

"I like when you lose control," she said.

Alex grimaced. "That's not what I meant, Sarah. You know what I mean. He pushed a lock of hair from her forehead.

"I know." She snuggled her back against him. "But I've missed this. I've been so afraid of losing you."

"I'm sorry, Baby."

"It'll be okay," she said. "You just need to stop getting so upset over things. Like at the park with Aiden. What do you think, a bomb going to go off in the children's playground?"

Her sarcasm prickled down his spine and he turned away. He couldn't tell her about Yusuf or

Williams. All the softness left him. "It's late. I have to feed the horses at Kevin's."

Sarah's voice peaked. "There you go again. What's wrong? What did I do?"

He threw off the covers and got out of bed. "Nothing. I gotta go." His back to her, shirtless, he stepped into his cammies.

He shrugged to shake off the self-disgust flooding through him as he felt her eyes on his back. She couldn't read his mind, but still, she probably guessed the things he'd done.

She couldn't see his jaw twitch, her attention focused on his flexing deltoids as she reached over and slid her hand over them. She grabbed his waistband and tried to pull him closer. "Come back to bed." She rose up, kneeling on the mattress, and wrapped her arms around him, pressing her body against his back. Her palms moved slowly over his bare chest.

Unaffected, he gathered his watch and wallet from the nightstand. "I gotta go." Unwelcomed images raced in his head and doused any lingering thirst that had stirred in his groin. The fucking guilt and horror ate like acid in his throat. If he didn't leave now he would vomit right in front of her. He pried her arms from his chest. "I gotta go. I'll call you later."

"What is wrong with you? You just get what you want and now you're off to drink with your war buddies?" She tossed the sheets out of her way and jumped from the bed. "Do what you have to do." She was yelling now. She grabbed her jeans and t-shirt, stormed into the bathroom, and slammed the door.

He stood, stared at the door. He let his eyes travel across the room. Without him at home to pick up after her, Sarah's clothes draped the chair in the corner while others adorned the bedpost. Several pairs of shoes peeked out from the bed skirt. The disarray fed his irritation.

"Get this place cleaned up. It looks like a war zone." He stomped out to his truck and burned rubber half way down the block before he pulled over and parked. He pounded his fist against the steering wheel. God, he hated himself. He hated his life.

He paused, catching a glimpse of Aiden's small cap on the floorboard. He lifted the boy's cover to his face. His fingers traced the embroidered Marine Corp emblem and he inhaled the little boy scent. He'd drop the hat off tomorrow after they both cooled down. He stomped the accelerator and headed for the Ponderosa. A couple of beers would take down the migraine creeping across his forehead.

Kevin's truck occupied its usual space. Alex parked alongside, stepped out and lit a cigarette. Deep drags of nicotine injected into his system before he reached the door and pinched out the fire. Two bikers leaned against their Harleys smoking something sweeter smelling. He jerked open the door and entered. By the time Alex reached Kevin at the bar,his eyes adjusted to the dimness. Another buddy, Dave, perched on the stool next to Kevin. Dave's blonde hair grew tight against his head. He wore a denim vest, no shirt. Tattoos covered his bared biceps like sleeves. Diego lay quietly at the base of his master's barstool. Alex came up behind his friend as Kevin motioned to the man on the stool next to him. "Alex, you remember Dave? He just got back."

Alex nodded. "How's it going?" He shook Dave's hand, then bent down and scratched Diego's ears. Dave had lived down the street from him when they were kids. He was five years older and married with two sandy-haired kids, a boy and a girl. Dave had joined the Marines about four years ago.

"It's going." Dave finished off his beer and stood. "You can sit here. I gotta head out."

"Keep your head down." Kevin said, and turned to Alex. "Dave's been home less than six months and already put his request in for another tour."

"I can't cope here." Dave said. "I want to get back in the action. I'll get another in-grade promotion and with it being my third tour and time-in, I'll get over three hundred more a month."

Alex listened as Dave counted off the perks of another tour. Reading Alex's mind, Kevin punched him. "What are you thinking? You got Sarah and Aiden to consider. What would Sarah say?"

"We still aren't getting along, she'd probably be happy to see me go. We could always use the money."

"Really? Have you talked to her? You need to talk to her."

"Yeah sure." Alex thought about the nights at the FOB, wrestling with his comrades, drinking, eating pizza, and swapping war stories. He missed his team. He missed the adrenaline pumping through his veins. He wanted to feel proud again, kick ass, and be part of the team. Being proud... he really missed that.

CHAPTER 19

Alex's gut tightened. The weeks had passed. He and Sarah had been separated two months which seemed like two years. He followed Kevin up the walk to the Fredrick's front door, afraid he might screw up his and Sarah's relationship more than it already was. He worried about triggers. Today was Aiden's first birthday.

Sarah had been going to counseling, and had become tolerant of his moods. Alex's counselor had told him to explain his triggers to her - sirens, helicopters, smells. The more Sarah understood, the less volatile their relationship became , but the uncomfortable tolerance in the air between them hung like an Iraqi woman's' hijab. They had not shared their bed since the day at the park. The tension he felt affected his work. His boss had warned many times to keep his temper in check and Alex realized that was becoming nearly impossible. . As his insecurities festered he had even begun to mistrust Kevin. Home ten months now, he still hardly slept, but he used the time to study until he had to go to work..

Kevin carried a pecan pie in one hand and rang the bell with the other, Diego sat obediently by his side. When the front door opened, Mr. Fredricks' bulk filled the entrance. "Come on in boys." His face softened as he gazed down on Diego. "You too, Diego." His father-in-law intimidated Alex, but he recalled what Sarah had told him about her father's issues. Monkey Man came to Alex's mind. The thought occurred that, like Monkey Man, Mr. Fredricks probably had his own secrets. He clasped his father-in-law's hand. "Good to see you, Sir."

"Everyone's in the kitchen. Go on in."

Festive banners looped around the windows and the aroma of a cake baking caused Alex to feel foolish that he couldn't relax. In the kitchen, Alex's mother and his sister, Arlene, each with spatulas in hand, huddled over Aiden's birthday cake. They turned in unison and rushed him. Spatulas raised high, arms spread, they encircled him in a group hug. Arlene, the first to release him, gave him a loving punch. "Good to see you, Bro."

His mother leaned back, arching her head up. "I've missed you, son. I wished we lived closer." She wiped her forehead with her free hand. "But the summers are so hot here."

Alex smiled at her. "You didn't complain about the weather when you were here for Thanksgiving. You'll have to split your time, spend your summers with Arlene and your winters down here with me."

His mother's brow furrowed and she rubbed his back. "I'm worried about you, Alex. What's happening with you and Sarah? You know Aiden needs you, having a father around is important. You remember how difficult a time you had after your father died."

"Mom, we're working on it. I just need some time." He pulled away.

His sister punched him again. "You'd better man up, Bro." She grabbed his hand and rubbed it over her protruding belly, "Your niece, Kaylee, here, needs her aunt, her uncle and her cousin."

He grinned. "Congratulations, Sis. Now I see what you two do during those long winter nights." He kissed her on the forehead. "Don't worry about me and Sarah. We've just got some things to work out, that's all."

Arlene was the next to greet Diego. She knelt down. "Who is this beautiful fella?" She rubbed Diego's ears and peered around to read his vest. "Service Dog, huh? I've heard about what these dogs do." She gazed up at her mother. "Doesn't your friend, Judy, have something to do with training these dogs?"

Alex's mother patted Diego. "Yes, she does. She is in Illinois right now. Her old high school sweetheart, Brad, invited her to stay on after she attended their 40th High School Reunion. They had dated seriously but broke up after graduation when she went to college in California." She looked up musingly, "That was forty years ago." She straightened up. "Judy's teen boyfriend, Brad, is now the chief of The Springfield Police Department. He never married." Alex's mother smiled as she recalled the romantic story. "At the reunion, since Judy's husband had passed away several years ago, Brad didn't hesitate to let her know he wanted to rekindle their relationship. After all these years, he's still in love with her."

Alex started to walk away. He didn't want to listen to fairy tale love stories.

His mother rushed on with her story. "So, it was like the right time for them, after forty years. Their relationship flourished, and they decided to partner up to build The K9s For Warriors Facility where they're now training dogs to be service dogs, like Diego here. Judy said the program had been Brad's dream. It's a win-win situation. It benefits both the prisoners and the veterans.

"Judy took a leave of absence from her grooming and training business here in California and went to Illinois to contribute her forty years of expertise in dog training. Brad, as Chief of Police handled the red tape to line up the prisoners who would participate in training. He even donated a section of his farm for the facility. When the dogs are finished with their training, Brad and Judy will select the wounded veterans who will receive the highly trained dogs. Judy says it takes almost two years to train a dog like Diego."

"That's right Mrs. March," Kevin said. "Diego was trained by inmates at the Women's Chino Prison. I met the woman who trained him. She was doing time for an armed robbery and looked like someone you wouldn't want to mess with, but when she had to say good bye to Diego, she cried. She'd trained him for over eight months and said that it was the most worthwhile thing she had ever done in her life."

Arlene rose and faced Alex. "Maybe you should get a dog, Bro." She punched Alex's arm. "Aiden would like a dog."

"There's a year waiting list." The subject irritated Alex and he turned to leave.

Mrs. Fredricks stepped forward and relieved Kevin of his mother's pecan pie. "You didn't have to bring anything," she said. "But I know your mom. Even from her vacation in the Bahamas, she insisted, right? I know she keeps a reserve in the freezer. I do love her pies. Don't forget to thank her for me." She hugged Kevin, kissed his cheek and knelt down to Diego. "I'm so glad you both came."

Before Alex could escape, Sarah entered the kitchen. He watched as she embraced Kevin. *Since when did she hug him like that?* He wanted to break every bone in her body, the body he loved to touch. Counseling had given them more understanding of one another, but they had lost their spontaneity and innocence. Hurt, fears, and responsibilities had washed out their bright red passion. Only the muted pink colors the therapist called maturity was left. Alex wondered if they would ever feel the passion again. What if they couldn't get it back?

Aiden squealed from his high chair interrupting his stinking thinking. He shoved his doubts into that over-crowed compartment of his brain labeled "later" and scooped up his son. He had to keep it together, especially today.

"Hey recruit. How about a big kiss for daddy?" The boy's mouth, smeared with mashed peas opened to belt out another excited squeal. Alex bent backwards as the baby lurched to kiss his daddy. "Later Jarhead. Let me wipe your mug." The happy baby's face reddened, and he bellowed out disapproval.

In less than thirty minutes, the picturesque table, full of food, became a half-eaten carnage of left overs.

At the end of the day, images of Aiden's face smeared with cake and icing, along with his parents' smiling faces, covered their Facebook wall, showing no evidence of the invisible issues with which the family struggled.

Invading thoughts of Yusuf's family and Sergeant Williams's family crept into the dining room, but Alex forced his focus back on Aiden. Tired from the day's events, the boy's eyes fluttered. His chin dropped to his chest, then bounced back up, as the baby's heavy lids fought the sandman.

"It looks like my little Marine needs some R and R." Alex glanced at Sarah and she nodded. "I'll put him down for his nap," he said.

After tucking in his son, and while the women finished in the kitchen, Alex joined Kevin and Mr. Fredricks in the den. CNN's Edward Murrow filled the TV screen as the newsman reviewed the schedules for the major football team's summer training.

Mr. Fredricks eyes never left the screen as he said, "There's talk that TBI is really prevalent in the NFL. I just read *League of Denial.* Have you boys read it? It's based on Mike Webster's career with the Pittsburgh Steelers, remember him?"

Alex turned and stared at Mr. Fredricks, surprised TBI, the term for traumatic brain injury, slid off his lips so easily.

"I remember him." Kevin said. "But I haven't read the book. An autopsy suggested Webster suffered a brain injury from the constant impacts of the game but I thought they decided his death was a heart attack?"

"Only because the NFL did their own study." Mr. Fredricks answered. "They concluded just last year that playing football did not damage the brain. I predict someday they're going to rue that decision."

The men continued watching the game, perhaps with a little less enthusiasm.

When the day concluded Alex kissed Sarah goodnight in the hall. They hugged stiffly. "I don't have to work tomorrow." Alex said." I'll be over early so you and your mom can go shopping."

"Thanks Alex."

How was it ever going to get better?

CHAPTER 20

Alex had stepped onto the tarmac unaware that, by itself, a young marriage with a new baby proved fertile grounds for nurturing stress and money problems. He wanted everything for his family, but working part time and going to school limited his dreams. Sarah had become the primary wage earner, weakening Alex's already fragile self-esteem. She was thrifty, content to allow Aiden to beat a wooden spoon on a metal pot and stack worn building blocks she found at a garage sale. "If I want to start my own business. I've got to save every penny," she said.

Not that he wanted money from her. He was getting by, but he regretted he couldn't lavish her and Aiden with gifts. Modest pearl earrings and a matching necklace was all he could afford for her birthday. When he gave them to her, she hugged him like she used to, and he dreamed of the past when life was simple. Her gifts for his birthday - a new paint ball gun and a running outfit. At a year old, Aiden had been easy to please with a popcorn popper push toy, a new set of blocks, and a pile of stuffed toys.

Alex passed his spring semester finals and realized he had achieved a 3.5 grade average - in spite of his insurmountable problems. He and Kevin celebrated at the Jungle Island Paint Ball Park, kicking ass until dark and then drinking at the Ponderosa until it closed.

"I can't believe we've finished a semester," Alex said as he pounded Kevin's back. "Maybe we'll make it after all."

"Sure we will." Kevin reached down and hugged Diego. "You and me boy. I couldn't have done it without you." The dog went everywhere with Kevin. Diego was a hit at Kevin's classes, a regular chick magnet. Kevin was more relaxed, even happier. Still, Kevin kept to himself, but Alex was okay with that. He figured Kevin, too, harbored too many subjects that were off limits.

"Another tour might not be so tempting, right Alex?" Kevin raised his beer to meet Alex's toast. "You're going to be a great detective," Kevin went on. "And with me a journalist – I can do ride-alongs while I research my New York Times bestselling novel." Their bottles clinked. "To the future."

Mornings and evenings, before work and classes, Miss Belle greeted Alex with a whinny, as he scooped up the oats into her pail. She never failed to swipe his cap while he groomed her. She had gained weight while Kevin's folks, who now, accustomed to the boys' assistance at the ranch, were on another cruise, this time to the Caribbean.

"I told you to hang in there." Alex talked to Miss Belle as the curry comb made rhythmic circles on the mare's withers. "The barn's always darkest before you open the barn door. Haven't you heard that?" He patted her rump as her head swung around, velvet lips extended to snatch his cap. He laughed and stepped back, careful not to trip on Spider Cat weaving between his legs. I'm becoming a regular Dr. Doolittle, he thought.

The animals asked no questions, yet they needed him. He thought of Kevin's bond with Diego. Alex had not brought up the service dog issue in a while, anyway, he was coping. He had received a couple of write-ups at work about his attitude, but he was making a renewed effort to control his temper. He wanted to keep his job at Bradley's Auto because the hours fit his school schedule. When he had enrolled for the summer semester, he was always on the edge of his anger. If the instructor made detrimental comments about the war, Alex was ready to explode. Didn't the school know that it was the military that insured their freedoms? And if he had to deflect one more question like, "Did you kill anyone?" Or one more statement like, "Why are you complaining, you volunteered, didn't you?" he was certain he would punch someone's lights out. The months rolled on.

The counselor at the vet center taught him to recognize his triggers. He still slept less than five hours, and constantly battled to control his rage. When he baby-sat Aiden, if Sarah came home late from work, his insecurities shifted into overtime. His mind presented doomsday scenarios, which usually included Sarah being mugged, or worse, having a clandestine rendezvous with another man. When she finally arrived home, arguments ensued. If they weren't arguing their conversations were reduced to the discussion of only necessary things. Sarah no longer cried. Worse, she portrayed aloofness and a sullen attitude. On good days they exchanged basic pleasantries and the months rolled on. Their separation neared the six month mark.

Alex paused from scooping the grain into Miss Belle's pail when his leg tickled from the phone's vibration. He pulled it from his pocket. "Sarah, what's up? Everything okay?" She never called this late.

Aiden squalled in the background, Sarah's high pitched voice barely audible. "Aiden cut his head open on the coffee table. We're on our way to emergency." She was crying now.

Alex's heart slammed against his chest. "Is he okay? I'll be right there."

"No! We're almost at the hospital. Meet us there."

Twelve months of images of guts and gore flashed into his mind. He steeled his muscles until no emotion dared leak out. Halfway to the hospital, he gained some kind of control and pulled himself back from Iraq.

In the hospital parking lot, he zeroed in on Sarah's car by his son's heart breaking cries. She hefted Aiden to her shoulder as Alex came up behind her. "I've got him." he said, and lifted Aiden from her grasp. "Go on in and give 'em a head's up." He sprinted behind her through the doors.

How many times had he done this before? Where was the helicopter? This was his son. His face froze in determination. This was his son. Two nurses rushed up.

"We'll take him, Sir."

"This is my son."

Fingers dug into his arms.

"Sir, you have to let go."

There was no room to think. Aiden's cries flooded his brain. His ears rang. He heard the copter's rotors. Whoosh, whoosh, whoosh. They would take him now and he would never know if he survived.

"He's my son. You're not taking him." He felt Sarah's hand on his shoulder and he jerked away. "Don't touch me! He's my son!"

The nurses nodded at one another and backed away. "Right this way, sir." They led him through the bowels of the hospital and into a room crowed with emergency monitors and a gurney. He laid Aiden gently on the cot and cooed over the boy's sobs as Sarah answered the older nurse's questions.

The younger nurse cleaned the cut. "He's going to be fine, Sir. He's just going to need some stitches." How many times had Alex said the same thing to one of his team? "How long you been home, Marine?....Sir?"

Alex pulled his focus from the bloody gash and met the nurse's calm controlled eyes with confusion. "Your cap, Sir." She pointed to the Marine Corps pin on his cap. "I was Army. A medic. Two tours."

"Twelve months, Ma'am."

Aiden's body quivered, weakened to short baby gasps.

The nurse held gauze against the gashing wound. "Press this to his head," she ordered. "The doctor will be in shortly."

Alex floated through the next several hours as if drugged. The nurses' orthopedic shoes squished-squished back and forth past the emergency room door. Patient's shouts and the quiet beeps of monitors accented soft whispers. Torturous hours dragged by before the doctor slipped in and expertly sewed the stitches while Alex pinned his son's small arms to the table. Aiden's wails pierced the hospital's deceptive hush. Alex glanced up at Sarah's anguished face but quickly turned away.

Aiden slept from exhaustion as his warrior father carried him to the car. Sarah stood aside while Alex strapped his son into the car seat, the small body still jerked from his whimpers, even in slumber. Alex straightened, closed the car door, and turned to Sarah. She wrapped her arms around his neck and pulled him close. "Oh Alex, I don't know what I would have done if..."

"It's okay." He patted her back. "It's okay. Everything's okay." He could smell her hair. Strawberries. "Get in." He opened the passenger door. "I'll get my truck tomorrow."

When they arrived at the house, Alex carried Aiden inside and tucked him in. The parents collapsed on the couch and Sarah curled up under Alex's arm. The hospital bill was not discussed. Moments passed before the other piece of Alex's heart beat evenly, and Sarah slept soundly on his shoulder. He gathered her up and carried her to the bedroom.

As he pulled off her shoes, she woke. "Don't go," she said, and drew him down to her. He lay down beside her, wrapping her in his arms until she, again, fell asleep. He listened to her level breathing and reviewed the night. He was her hero, but she didn't know how close he had come to losing it....one more time. The nurse recognized his panic. Sarah saw his valor, but Alex knew his failure. He eased off the bed, checked on Aiden. Rather than call Kevin he used the opportunity to burn of his churning emotions and jogged the five miles back to his solitary life where he couldn't hurt anyone.

Kevin maneuvered his pickup through the light morning traffic to the hospital to drop off Alex at his truck. Alex rode shotgun, hyper vigilant, focused on everything. Diego sat between them studying the route. Alex thought of the bomb sniffing dog back home in Iraq, Detect, they called him, short for Detector. An amazing dog. *Did I just say, back home in Iraq?*

"How much did the ER cost you?"

"They hit my card with five hundred, but warned me more will be trickling in over the next thirty days." *Did I say 'back home' out loud or just think it?*

"Are you good for it?" Kevin glanced at Alex.

"I don't know, man. I just bought Sarah the Honda. She needed something reliable. The down payment took all our savings so we could keep the payments low." *Another tour would solve everything.*

"My folks might be able to help you out."

"No, man. I can't do that. I'm going to sign up for another tour. I've made up my mind." *There. I said it out loud.* "I'm going to tell Sarah today."

"What the hell are you thinking?" Kevin slammed on the brakes as he pulled up next to Alex's truck in the hospital parking lot. His angry eyes bore into Alex's. Or was it worry? "You can't do that to Sarah! What will she say?"

"She won't be happy, but it'll be for the best. She thinks I'm doing great, but she doesn't know. I almost lost it, Kevin. Right in the emergency room. If I had....God! I just can't stop this shit in my head!" His muscles flexed. He made a fist and pounded the dash. Diego nuzzled his arm.

"I gotta go," Alex said, as he pushed open the door and jumped out. "Thanks for the ride."

Kevin squealed the tires and sped away. The burnt rubber hovered in a cloud of blue as Alex yanked open his truck door and climbed in.

Fuck Kevin.

CHAPTER 21

He parked his truck and went in the house. Before the screen slammed shut behind him Sarah met him at the door and leapt into his arms. Her hair still smelled of strawberries. He held her tight. *Oh God, he was going to miss her.*

"After last night I realized we can't keep on like this," she said. She pulled back and looked up at him. "I want you to move back in. Maybe none of this would've happened if you'd been here." She caught her breath.

His body reacted to the feel of hers, and the hope in her words, but he placed his hands on her shoulders and gently pushed her back. "Are you sure?"

"We've been doing better. Don't you think I'm more supportive? I understand what you're going through. I can do this. Mom and Dad made it." Her eyes begged. "I can do this."

"Sure you're doing better, Honey. But I'm no better." He hadn't expected this. His heart skipped a beat with surprise and then pounded with yearning and hope. But his brain argued. *You'll only hurt her again. Maybe next time you'll hurt Aiden, too.*

"You're just upset, Sarah. I'm not any better. I don't want to hurt you or Aiden. I'm going to sign up for another tour." *Had he said it out loud?*

She jumped away as if he were on fire. "No!"

He had said it out loud.

"You can't do that!" Her fists grabbed his bleached white t-shirt, pulled him back to her. Black mascara tears soaked the linen with indelible smudges. "You won't hurt us. I trust you," she begged.

His heart beat out of control. His pulse throbbed against his throat. His arms tingled, his fingers numbed. He was bleeding out right in front of her. His mind blanked out, he quit searching for a way out, content to give up. "I've already decided," he said. "Anyway we need the money. I have an appointment with my commander tomorrow after my counseling session." He tried to pull away from her grasp.

Her fists sprang open. She released his shirt, marked with stains that would never wash out. He fell back. She stood in front of him, hands up as if he aimed a gun at her. "Really, Alex? You're just going to give up? You're quitting?"

"I'm doing this for you and Aiden!" She cringed at the volume of his voice. He took a deep breath, lowered his voice. "I don't know what else to do, another tour will solve everything."

"Yeah. And you could come home with no legs, or worse, in a body bag. No Alex, you can't do this. You can't do this to Aiden. What about a dog? I thought you were getting a dog?"

"It's a year waiting list. I gave up on that idea. Another tour is the only way."

Her chest flushed in anger as she paced the small yellow kitchen. She ran her fingers through her hair then stopped abruptly, and turned toward him. Like lasers, her eyes zeroed in on his. "You know what? Do what you have to do. I don't care anymore, either." She turned away. "I didn't think I married a quitter. Get out."

He couldn't move.

"She spun back around and faced him. "I said get out!" The intensity of her anger jarred him. Her eyes flashed with pain. Unable to move his leaden arms to reach for her, he turned and stumbled out the door. His body, his will drained out. It was over. The screen door slammed shut behind him.

Alex drove. Sarah didn't realize the depth of his failures. He was more than a quitter. She didn't know about Williams or Reikert or Yusuf. To Sarah he was only an unfeeling bastard. She didn't know he was a coward, cringing helplessly on a roof top. Alex didn't ever want his son to discover who his father really was. He drove and drove until he reached the lookout over Lake Elsinore. The sun set on the valley twenty-five hundred feet below as he parked and climbed out of his truck. Alex thought of the old mare, Miss Belle. Kevin worked late tonight. The feeding couldn't be pushed off on Kevin.

Was Kevin still his buddy? Had Kevin written him off too? Had he managed to poison every relationship that mattered? He leaned against the truck's grill, his legs crossed at his ankles, and lit a cigarette. He never smoked in Iraq. Did that mean the hell-hole-sand- trap was good for his health? He sneered at his own joke and laughed out loud. The venomous scorn evaporated as the sarcastic chuckle plunged over the mountain's edge.

The sun sank behind him as he gazed out on the valley below. Why couldn't any one understand, another tour was the only answer? Kevin should get it, but he had a dog now. Alex considered the interaction between Kevin and Diego. When the bartender at the Ponderosa had popped the cork on a bottle of champagne, Kevin had frozen, locking eyes with Alex's, and they both poised in combat mode. Diego had jumped up, laid his front paw on Kevin's lap, and poked his nose under his arm. The moment was over before it had a chance to drag them back to some haji village roof top, shooting a thousand rounds of ammo a minute at illusive fucking shadows. Diego had grounded him.

Alex uncrossed his legs and climbed back in his truck. He wouldn't last twelve months waiting for a service dog. His only choices were to die here as a suicide, or in Iraq as a hero. Maybe when he got back from the next tour, Sarah would calm down. Since counseling, she was more understanding. She always tried to comfort him when he lost control, but that only angered him more. Sarah shouldn't have to deal with his shit. She deserved better. Her offers of encouragement humiliated and enraged him. He fired up the truck and revved the engine. He'd go by and talk to her tomorrow after his counseling appointment. *I'll get her to understand.*

He jammed the accelerator to the floorboard and gravel spewed across the parking lot. He barreled out onto Ortega Highway. Adrenaline pulsed when the truck tires squealed around the first curve, inches from the deadly drop. He eased off. They grabbed, and he floored the accelerator again, laughing at the snaking road and enjoying the lethal thrill all the way down the mountain.

The addicting torment of the ride ended when he reached the city limits. Kevin turned into the ranch's long drive, slowed the truck to a crawl and parked – maybe for the last time – in front of the small bunk house. Depression sank into his bones and made them ache. Spider Cat uncurled from the rocker on the porch and trotted toward his truck. Miss Belle's whinny called from the barn as he slid out of the cab. He was so tired - tired of trying to survive. Tomorrow he met with his recruiting officer.

He trudged to the barn, Spider Cat leading the way, tail pointed up, straight as an arrow. Alex swung the barn door open and twilight flooded inside, lighting up the veil of dust in the air. Miss Belle snickered and tossed her head. He filled the mare's pail and took extra time grooming her. Again he thought, maybe for the last time. With circular motions he brushed to the crunching rhythm of her grinding jaws. Like a metronome, her tail switched back and forth.

Sarah and Kevin, even the mare and the cat, all needed what he couldn't give – dependability - dependability that only seemed to exist in Iraq. Tomorrow couldn't come soon enough. He finished the chores and headed back to the bunkhouse. As he slid the bolt across the door and barricaded himself inside, he took a deep breath and turned. Spider Cat's yellow eyes penetrated, as if questioning his judgment.

CHAPTER 22

Alex returned Spider Cat's stare with a glare of his own. Failing the competition, the warrior surrendered to the bed, stretched out, his hands behind his head. The feline sprinted across the bedspread, settled onto Alex's chest and nuzzled against the veteran's unshaven beard, purring loudly. Alex peered past the cat, out the window, and studied a black bird that cawed as it swayed on a limb, its dark form nearly the shade of the approaching nightfall. The bird took flight and disappeared. The raven's flapping wings jarred the barren limb it perched upon, and the branch shook and squeaked against the window's glass. One remaining leaf clung to the twig. The multi-colored remnant danced to the disturbance, released its hold, and then, it too, fluttered out of sight.

Alex had been away from his unit twelve months. His unit, who needed him. Every hour they faced life and death. Two of his team mates had come home, one in a body bag. The emotional pull to join them was constant, like gravity. Good times pranced in his mind as he lay on the bed and ran his hand over Spider Cat's soft fur. The camaraderie in the FOB. Laughing at the sick, satanic jokes about death and dying. Wrestling and jamming until dawn. A cold slice of pizza crammed in his pocket, flown over from an alien world. Skyping Sarah and Aiden…

Sarah and Aiden. The six months of separation from his family only enhanced the emotional allure for Iraq, making it even more seductive. His body sank deeper into the mattress and slipped into a dreamlike trance.

A lifeline dangled from a copter. He heard the thump- thump and roar of the rotors, even felt their gusts. Hand over hand, he lifted himself to safety from the fire fight below. A hand clasped his and pulled him into the dark bowels of the copter. Safely inside, he caught his breath and looked up. An insurgent's cold empty eyes bore into his.

Alex's eyes flew open. He flung Spider Cat from his chest, rose and began to pace. The demonic visions never stopped. They came unbidden. He shivered to shake off the specter.

Only when he was awake did he recall the esprit de corps. Was the insurgent in the copter a real memory? Did the enemy control his conscious memories in order to lure him back to face his death? Or, were these phantoms he dreamed powered by some goodness in his life, created to warn him?

He continued to pace. Tomorrow he walked point. Whatever his actions, tomorrow two teams would be affected – his team in Iraq and his team here.

Outside the gingham curtains, twilight faded fast. He was so tired. He sank back down on the bed. Sarah wanted him home. Aiden needed his daddy. They were everything to him. They were what he fought for. Their images kept him strong throughout a firefight. Yet here at home, their goodness and innocence only fed his guilt and shame, alienating him from what he missed and yearned for most- love and acceptance.

A dog might have saved him. He had watched Diego work with Kevin. He envied Kevin and the change in him. Now, his buddy was like the others who hated him too and Kevin's concern for Sarah irritated Alex. She's not his business. *Is she?*

Alex woke fully dressed. Another morning, like so many others in the last twelve months. No, not today. Today he walked point. What he planned to do today affected everyone in his life, his family and his unit. Still numb from disturbing sleep, he splashed cold water to his face. Exhaustion and depression had allowed him to sleep late. He looked at the clock. Only fifty-eight minutes to feed the horses and arrive at his appointment with Mark Parrish. He rushed through his chores and was on the road in thirty.

He sprinted across the parking lot and rushed into the vet center. Signing in, he bent to sit down just as Mark opened his door and ushered him in. Relieved the session was one-on-one, Alex took a seat, drew in a deep breath, and began. "Sir,…"

"Before you begin Alex, I have some news." Mark pulled a folder from the stack on his desk.

"Yes, Sir?"

Mark sat straighter in his chair. Was the counselor nervous or excited? Alex squirmed, perspiration trickled down his back.

"Your application for a service dog came through. An organization called K-9s For Warriors Program, based in Illinois, has offered to provide you with a dog. You must have friends in the right places. You've been bumped to the top of their waiting list. Congratulations, Marine."

Alex did not move. *How could this have happened?*

The therapist read the wounded Marine's stunned expression. "Judy Howard is a friend of yours?"

The name penetrated his shock. "Yes, she's a friend of my mother's and Sarah's parents. She owns the pet grooming salon here in Sun City, but…?"

"Well, Ms. Howard has been in Illinois the past year as a consultant in the training and operation of the K9s For Warriors Facility. You will be receiving one of their first dogs to graduate from that facility." Mark smiled broadly. "Like I said Marine, you have friends in the right places. They've scheduled a flight on Southwestern at oh-eight hundred tomorrow. You'll be in a training program in I Illinois with the dog for the next two weeks."

A torrent of images flooded Alex's mind, each wave screamed with contradicting emotions. His head spun.

Panic: The insurgent in the copter let go of the rope.

Fear: Diego's big eyes stared into his soul.

Hope: A misty blue aura clouded around Sarah. She led Aiden by the hand as they fell into a faceless Marine's arms.

Freedom: Rockets soared in the air like a fourth of July celebration. They lit up the horizon and illuminated an image of himself. He was tossing his cap up in the air on graduation day, his brave dog by his side, and his team mates stood at attention in the background.

Mark came around to the front of his desk. "Congratulations, Alex."

The movement brought him back to the room. He stood. "Yes sir. Thank you Sir." His hand took the folder Mark held out.

Mark was shaking his hand. "I can't wait to meet your new team member. Come by as soon as you get back."

A Team member? Someone to watch his back?

CHAPTER 23

Alex laid the folder on the dash, fired up the truck, and threw it into drive. It lurched, the tires squealed, and he peeled out of the lot.

This changed everything. When Sarah got the news, she would forgive him for hurting her - one more time. That's all he needed, one more chance. With a dog he'd be back under the wire. His mind wiped out his Iraqi memories. Instead his brain ran scenes of himself, Sarah and Aiden in the park, of snuggling on the couch with the two pieces of his heart tucked under each of his arms, of Aiden's first day at school, of the grand opening at Sarah's hair salon, of him driving a squad car. The mental video played over and over like a hit song that he knew the words to– easy, feel good, romantic music. He would tell Sarah he loved her and he wanted to come back home. He was tired of being alone. Would she forget her anger and tell him she forgave him? Did she miss him too? Would they get that old time feeling and laugh and cry together?

He slammed on the brakes as he negotiated the turn onto their street. His head swayed with the lightness of his mood. When was the last time his heart beat with such hope for the future? He didn't realize how depressed he had been until right now. No wonder she didn't want him in her bed. When was the last time his world swirled from the dizziness of excitement to see her? She would see him now, full of optimism and desire and he would sweep her up and fill her with his fire.

He completed the turn, stomped on the gas, but in the middle of the street, immediately slammed on the brakes. Kevin's truck sat in front of Sarah's house. Maybe it wasn't Kevin's. Yes, it was.

Sarah's and Kevin's profiles appeared in the truck's back window, poised to kiss. Sarah's hair draped over Kevin's arm which wrapped around her shoulder. Alex couldn't breathe. His head hammered and his knuckles cracked as they clutched the wheel.

Just a peck on the cheek, wasn't it? Did she promise more? Did Kevin promise never to hurt her? Did he tell her he understood how lonely she was? Where was Diego? Evidently Kevin had found someone better to bond with. Where was Aiden?

Alex punched the dash and bore down on the horn. The blare invaded his internal inquisition. The couple's moment interrupted, the two looked up. A cloud of blue, rubber-smelling smoke engulfed Alex's squealing truck as it barreled toward the couple. He saw the surprise and the fear in their eyes as he neared impact. He saw Sarah's mouth opened to release a scream which he didn't hear because, at the last moment, he swerved just as the speedometer hit sixty. He laughed in spite of the burning rage that could not be extinguished by the hot tears now blinding his vision. He smashed the brake pedal to the floor. Screeching. Or was it Sarah's scream? He yanked the wheel, leaned into the truck's spin, and dropped it into low gear. The engine choked, and, again, he crammed the accelerator to the metal. The lovers' bodies scrambled inside the cab as he approached, fully engaged, to ram into the rear.

Aiden's small head peeked over Sarah's shoulder. Warning alarms fired off in his head like the sirens at the FOB as Sarah frantically tried to slide herself and her son toward the passenger door.

The joy of revenge dove into a tail spin, out of control. Boot camp trained Alex to control his panic, use his rage. He slammed down the brake pedal and yanked the wheel. The truck rallied, screamed, and spun again, reversing direction. Alex floored the accelerator and sped away from the adulteration without looking back.

He burst into the bunkhouse. A high pitched siren still pulsated in his ears. *Shit.* The shrill sound drowned out the screams of fury and madness bleeding out from his excruciating invisible wound. *Gotta keep moving.* He rustled through the papers in the small dresser drawer for a note pad and pencil and scribbled a note, *Mr. and Mrs. K., Thank you for helping me out. I have found other arrangements.*

Spider Cat studied Alex's frantic movements from his perch on the window sill as Alex pulled his duffle from under the bed and carried the bag to the bathroom. With one sweep, he shoved the toiletries in on top of his skivvies. He left the sweet smelling towels and soap and scanned his quarters for any evidence of his presence, his eyes stopped on the cat.

He had walked away from comrades bleeding out in the sand, watched the medics shove their lifeless bodies into the copter without ever revisiting the carnage in his mind… or his heart…he had always maintained control…until now.

He approached the cat, who gingerly reached out his paw for the treat he had trained Alex to supply. Alex dug his fingers into his t-shirt pocket, ignoring the tattered glossy. He pinched out a couple morsels and laid them on the window ledge. As the cat examined Alex's offer, Alex hefted the duffle's strap over his shoulder, took two long strides, and vacated the quarters.

Keep moving. They might have called the cops. He'd seen his buddies arrested for less. He had sabotaged what little was left of any relationship with his two best friends, Kevin and Sarah. He always thought he would gain control of the demons that haunted him... until now.

He came close to killing the only two people in his life who mattered. He might go to jail. How many of his buddies were doing time because they'd lost control? He threw his truck into reverse, turned around and accelerated down the long drive.

In the pasture, Miss Belle raised her head and whinnied as his road dust clouded around her. Uncontrollable sobs and agonizing moans that Alex could no longer deny, filled the cab. He rubbed his eyes. Too late, too little, too much. Too late to go back. Too little left to care about. Too much.

All this time he'd been blind, delusional. He should have seen. He should have known how it would all turn out. If he had just surrendered, admitted his fears and doubts, admitted he was at the end. But he was a Marine, wasn't he? No survivors! No surrender! Once a Marine, always a Marine. Semper Fi and all that shit. They'd have to carry him off in a body bag before he'd surrender.

He handed the fee to the ranger at the campground kiosk. "One night," he said.

The woman nodded and held up her palm. "No sir. This one's on me." She said. "Marines, First Division, Fifth Regiment."

'"That's not necessary Ma'am."

"No Sir. I insist."

Ashamed by her offer of respect and pride, he didn't make eye contact. He kept his head down and placed the bills back in his wallet. "Thank you, ma'am. Carry on."

The campground was crowded compared to his stay a lifetime ago. He made his way to the less occupied tent area, parked in a secluded site and turned off the ignition. He breathed in deeply and exhaled slowly. Again. And again. His heart rate slowed and he concentrated, relaxing his muscles.

Why hadn't he seen the signs between Kevin and Sarah? They had been there. At the birthday party in the kitchen. Breathe in...and out. And at the paint ball park. They wrestled in fun until Kevin made a joke about Alex's manhood. Already insecure from the separation, the play fight turned ugly like an ambush in the night. The best friends fisted up and charged like mad dogs. Their buddies pulled them apart, and even though they shook hands, even pounded fist, the unease lingered. Alex's twisted heart throbbed. *Breathe in, breathe out.*

He jumped out of the truck and sprinted onto the trail beside the campsite. He ran until his legs burned, then dropped to the ground and did push-ups until his arms, too, were on fire. An hour later he plodded back to his truck. Campfires and lanterns cast shadowy figures across his path. The sun had set. He reached into the truck bed and lifted the ice chest's lid, grabbing the last three beers bobbing in the melted ice water. He climbed into the cab and stretched out across the bench seat. He propped his head against the passenger arm-rest and jammed his jacket behind his neck.

The strain of the workout cleared his mind. The heaviness which shadowed him for the past twelve months, lightened. He had been such a fool. He had wasted so much time. How much had he lost insisting he didn't have PTSD? *Do you have to lose everything?* He knew of comrades that were homeless or doing time because of their invisible disease. That's what everyone was calling it now, the invisible disease. He tried to laugh at the irony. It was not invisible to him.

Maybe there was hope for him. *You're sleeping in your truck, dude, really?* He popped the cap on the third beer and threw the warm liquid back in three big gulps. A weak smile at his own joke made his face feel as if it would crack. He focused on the dog he would get. His body and mind exhaled. Whatever fight that remained in him, died. He surrendered.

Morning peeked over the horizon, tracing the black hills in a yellowish grey outline. Alex checked his watch. Two hours before his flight at Ontario. He rubbed his palm over his beard's stubble. He'd shave at the airport. He pulled his phone from his vest, two missed calls, one from Sarah and one from Kevin. No bars. He shoved the cell deep into his jean pocket, sat up and climbed out of the truck. A nest of rabbits in the clearing froze on hind legs and studied him as he moved out.

He ran, listening to the pounding of his boots as they beat against the dusty path. Mornings were his favorite time of the day, before the world woke up. He focused on the rhythm of his breathing, easy, steady, in control. The heat in his legs pushed him on and he picked up the pace. Cool air filled his lungs.

His torso swayed to the cadence. His arms pumped out frustrated, desperate energy. He ran harder. He demanded his mind concentrate on the intensity of the PT, but it refused. It was out of control, sprinting off the path like a coyote with that last image of Sarah and Kevin in its jaws. Like the coyote, his brain violently shook the image. Back and forth, back and forth. Distorted, the spectacle blurred into an obscene, adulterated movie.

He had blown it big time, this time. He had blown it, like he had with Williams. He'd pushed Sarah over the edge. He'd killed her love. It should have been him, in Sarah's arms. He'd killed Williams. It should have been him that had looked over the wall. After Williams was taken out, Alex always insisted on walking point. It should have been him. It should have been him. His head blown off. He'd blown everything. His boots pounded the earth. He ran harder. He passed the camp host space, but it was not Monkey Man's rig.

He was on fire. His legs, his arms, his lungs. He ran harder. Train hard, fight hard, drink hard. Sarah hated his drinking. He ignored her glare when he reached for the second six pack because he knew he had no control. Yet, he felt in control. Like in his dream, when the insurgent dangled the rope from the copter. Now he knew, if he pulled himself in, he'd be killed, yet if he let go, he'd die in the firefight. But he was going to have to let go while he was still strong enough to fight.

The campsites fluttered to life as his boots pounded by. A man nodded, still in his PJs, as he monitored his dog's sniffing investigation of his campsite. The dog barked as Alex loped by, his workout now in the cooling off stage.

He'd fight to the death. That was what he was trained to do. No surrender. Only two options remained. The dog or another tour. He'd get on the plane, go get the dog, give it a try. Everyone wanted him to get the dog. If it didn't work, he'd do the tour.

He raised his arm and wiped the sweat from his brow as he approached his truck. Braking in front of the vehicle, he leaned down and gripped his thighs. Heavy breathing dried his mouth and he licked his lips. When he caught his breath, he rose up, and lifted the lid on the cooler. Empty cans floated in the melted ice. He slammed the cover closed. He'd suck it up. He did a silent 'ooh rah' and jerked open the truck door.

Traffic to the airport was heavy but he arrived in time to declare his gun, check his bag, and find his gate. He washed up in the restroom, shaved, and was dabbing his face with a paper towel when the cell phone's vibration grabbed at his gut. He didn't want to talk to anyone, couldn't. He marched out to the waiting area, took a seat, legs spread, back to the wall.

He should have asked Kevin what you had to do to get the dog. He was sure they didn't just hand over the dog on its leash and say, "Here you go buddy. Have a great life." But he couldn't call Kevin. Not now. Maybe now is the time. I can't kill him with me here and him there. Where was he? Still comforting Sarah?

"Flight 3049 now boarding."

Fuck it. Time to move out. Step it up, Jarhead.

He boarded and found his seat. He was getting a dog.

CHAPTER 24

Judy Howard was the friend in the right place, at the right time. Nearing sixty, she didn't show signs of slowing down. She waited at the gate, chatting quietly to the man next to her whom Alex assumed was the boyfriend, Brad. Alex knew her only as his mother's friend, who operated the pet grooming and training facility at home in California, and who had lost her husband to cancer a few years ago.

Alex passed through the airport gate. He wore khakis and shouldered his duffle with ease. Pausing, he scanned the passenger waiting room. He processed every person standing, sleeping, or sitting, then moved to the baggage area where he locked eyes with Judy.

He moved toward her with the presence of a warrior, no longer the boy she remembered. His khakis hung loose over his intense body. Every muscle announced readiness. When he approached her, his eyes softened, and he said, "Hello, ma'am. Thank you for meeting me. You didn't have to. And thank you for what you are doing for me." He paused. "I don't know what to say…."

She held up her hand. "It's no problem, Alex, your family and Sarah's helped me out once when I really needed it." She smiled and wrapped her arms around him in a warm hug. When he stiffened, she stepped back, and turned to the man standing beside her, who stood six inches over her head. He wore jeans and a t-shirt under a leather jacket. "Alex, I would like you to meet Police Chief Brad Jones. He's instrumental in starting the K-9 For Warriors Program."

Alex turned, assessing the Chief as he clasped his hand. They shook with forceful, steel grips which jerked their shoulders. "Nice to meet you, Sir," Alex said.

"Welcome to Illinois. It's an honor to meet you, Marine."

"Yes, Sir." Alex scanned the throngs of people constantly moving past them.

Brad read the tautness in Alex's face and said, "Let's head out. We have a car waiting."

On the drive from the airport, spurts of polite small talk sprang up amongst the trio. "How are Sarah and Aiden?" Judy asked.

"Good."

"Aiden must be getting big?"

"Yes, Ma'am. I can't believe how much the boy has grown."

"I understand you've been in counseling?" The Chief asked.

Alex exhaled a breath he must have been holding the entire flight. "Yes, Sir. Counseling's okay. I hated it at first but the psych who moderates the group is really good at explaining things. I'm beginning to understand my triggers."

"With a dog you're going to be fine." The Chief said. "These dogs work wonders."

Judy leaned against the passenger door and said, "Of course this is our first litter. There were four golden retriever puppies, two males, Rocky and Boise, and two females, Daisy and Masada." Her eyes lit up as she said their names. "For the first twelve months of their lives they each had a puppy raiser whose intense assignment included twelve months of training, twenty four hours, seven days a week. The puppy went everywhere with its trainer. I was Masada's puppy raiser and Brad raised Daisy." She looked at Brad and smiled. Alex could feel the connection between the two. "When the puppies reached a year old, they went to the prison. There we assigned them to prisoners whom Brad and I handpicked. The sterile prison environment, with its steady routine, is ideal in order to perfect and refine the dogs' obedience skills even more."

Alex nodded. "My friend..." His mouth twisted. "has a service dog. It was trained by a woman inmate."

"Oh so you know a little about what the dogs go through?"

"Well, not really. Kevin hasn't told me much." *He's too busy consoling my wife.*

"These four puppies, grown dogs now, are at the end of twenty months of this intense training. They are ready to leave us and become responsible for the life of a veteran like you, who will depend of it for emotional, and sometimes, even physical support."

Sadness flashed across Judy's face. She glanced at Brad, again. "Masada and Daisy have changed our lives in the last twenty months, just as Boise and Rocky have affected their puppy raisers. And all four of the dogs have made a difference in the inmates' lives." Her face brightened again. "Boise was the only puppy not to graduate as a service dog, but we have assigned him to a position more suitable for his personality. I am confident all do what they are trained to do. And I am certain your service dog will change your life."

Judy passed the rest of the trip relating her experiences with Masada. Before Masada's eyes even opened, Judy had nurtured the pup, rubbing her tummy and becoming a constant presence in the dog's life. She had been there every step of the way as Masada grew from a bumbling, roly-poly ball of scraggly fur, who tripped over her own paws, into a graceful, confident, eighty pound service dog whose flowing golden coat glistened in the sun. Judy spoke of her heartache as Masada endured her first experience with separation when Judy left her with her prison trainer, Roy, to complete her six months of prison life. "Now, I hope Masada will recover, once again, from the emotional loss of being taken from Roy."

Judy bragged about how Masada had coasted through the year and a half of training as if she were born to become a service dog. Two days from now, Masada and her two littermates, would select a veteran with whom they would spend the rest of their lives together.

The last couple of miles to the facility, the three rode in silence, each lost in their unexpressed doubts.

Standing just inside his room at the K9s For Warriors facility, Alex hung in the doorway as the Chief pointed out the features of his new quarters for the next two weeks.

"This is your own private patio," the Chief explained. Sunlight glinted off his badge as he slid open the glass door. "You can smoke out here, not in the facility." A small table and two chairs huddled in the corner. Ivy crawled up the trellis, carrying red and gold leaves that shivered in the cool October air. The Chief stepped back into the room and pointed to a hotel-sized refrigerator. "Snacks and drinks here, even a sandwich if you get hungry in the middle of the night. Unlike the hotels, these are free. Let us know what you prefer and we'll try to provide it." The chief's eyes fell down to Alex's trembling hands. "No alcohol on the grounds."

Alex flushed and shoved his hands in his pockets. "Yes, Sir."

"Call me Brad. We're informal here. Tomorrow, two more vets will be flying in. We'll have an orientation Monday morning, eight sharp, to explain the schedule for the next two weeks. At that time you'll meet and receive your service dog. So, for now, make yourself comfortable. "

The chief ran his hand over the bedspread, embroidered with the Marine Corps emblem that matched a throw pillow "This will be your home for the next two weeks as you and your new team member get to know each other." *Team member.* Brad moved toward the door to leave, paused, and turned to Alex. "Judy and I would like you to be our guest for dinner tonight."

The invitation sounded like an order. "Yes, Sir."

"Please, call me Brad." He repeated, this time with a small smile. "We'll come by for you at six. Congratulations, Marine. You are very lucky to have a friend like Ms. Howard."

"Yes, Sir, Chief Jones, Brad sir, Sir, thank you, Sir." Alex shook the Chief's hand vigorously, "Thank you." The chief exited the room.

Alone, Alex slumped down next to his duffle on the bed. After a moment, he grabbed the bag, shoved it into the small closet, and smoothed the spread. His eyes traveled over every detail in the room, from the hand embroidered pillow, to the Marine Corps flag standing in the corner. The room reflected the Corps' colors. The gray drapes bordered in gold brushed across a polished wood floor. He pulled the curtains half closed.

Grateful he was alone, he stood in the middle of the room. He searched for words that might express how he felt, if asked sometime, say a year from now, ten years from now. He wanted to remember this. He wanted to remember it all. The loneliness of the past twelve months. The isolation of being away from his team who understood him. The agony of existing stateside among civilians who did not understand, and to which, no explanation would ever be possible.

He wanted to remember this moment, this room, and the people he might never meet who were responsible. If all this was created for a defeated jarhead like him, a man who had lost everything... his dignity, his purpose, his family..., all this they had created because they believed a dog could change his life. Should he dare hope? The words of the Marine Prayer, memorized so long ago as a boy, filled with wonder and ambition, flooded into his mind. *Will this dog help me to, again, face my fellow Marines, my loved ones, and Thee without shame or fear?*

CHAPTER 25

Sitting out on his small patio, Alex barely heard the soft rap on his door. He pinched out his cigarette and laid it in the ashtray instead of his military habit of slipping the butt into his pocket. He grabbed his cap, smiled at Miss Belle's faint teeth marks on its bill, and opened the door.

"Ready?" Judy wore black Jeans and a light leather jacket over a rust colored silk blouse. Earrings and an angora scarf matched the blouse. Her salt and pepper hair, Alex noticed, matched the Chief's, but hers curled at her neckline.

Alex fingered the collar of his pinstriped shirt under his blazer. How long had it been since he worried about his appearance? "I wasn't sure how to dress. Should I have worn a tie?"   "You look great. Judy smiled and held out her arm for Alex. "These days it's called the casual-smart look. Brad's waiting in the car. We have reservations at the steakhouse downtown."

As Alex opened the car door, Judy said, "You boys can ride up front. I'll sit in the back seat." She pushed the seat forward to slip into the back.

Alex reached in and blocked her. "Ladies sit up front. I'll sit back there."

"Are you sure? You won't be cramped?"

"I've ridden on the hard-assed seat of a hummer, crammed in the back with my knees to my chin. This will feel like a limo ride.' He slipped in with a nimbleness that belied his size.

The log cabin style restaurant would have felt warm and inviting if Alex had not been so nervous. They passed a well-stocked bar as the hostess, dressed in period clothing from the Abe Lincoln era, showed them to a quiet corner booth. A waiter, wearing a black stove pipe hat, promptly appeared with menus.

"Good evening Chief," he said and focused on Alex. "Would your guest like something from the bar while you're waiting?"

Brad looked up from the menu. "Judy and I will have coffee. How about you Alex? Anything from the bar?"

The Chief's eyes felt like an M16's bead on his forehead. The air from the overhead fan brushed cool against Alex's sweaty temple. He hadn't had a drink since he left California. Oh eight hundred until …he glanced at his watch - eighteen hundred. Ten hours. When had he gone that long, except when on a mission?

Mission Service Dog. "No. Thank you, Sir." He couldn't remember when he felt so out of place, wondering if he fit in. "Coffee will be fine."

"So, tell me all about Aiden," Judy said. "How old is he now?"

Alex's smile felt stiff. "He's almost sixteen months. He's walking, running really. He never stops. His favorite lullaby is the Marine Corps Anthem and he still sucks his fingers, but everyone says he'll grow out of it. And he loves to play the drums on Sarah's pots and pans." He took a deep breath, forgetting his discomfort. "You should have seen him at his birthday party. Cake crumbs and icing all over his face. He's got little cammie PJ's and a cap with the Marine Corps insignia." Alex pulled out his phone and touched the screen. "Here's a cute one in the wading pool. Oh, and this one's last Christmas." Suddenly aware and embarrassed of his gushing report, he quickly shoved the phone back in his pocket.

After coffee was served and they had ordered, Brad leaned back, resting his arm over the back of the booth. "How did you and Sarah meet?" His deep voice spoke slow and easy, disguising the inquisition that Alex figured this was.

"We were high school sweethearts. Once I set eyes on her, I knew she was the one." Alex laughed, then sobered as he remembered his present dcpressing circumstances. He fidgeted with the silver ware. "We've been separated for six months, Sir. I don't think we're going to get back together."

Brad dropped his arm down around Judy's shoulder, hugging her. "I fell in love with this woman forty years ago. It took that long for her to figure out I was the one. " Brad gazed down at her and smiled. When she blushed, he looked back at Alex. "Don't give up the fight."

Alex wasn't going to admit Sarah was already in the arms of his best friend. His dinner partners seemed so hopeful.

The conversation lightened as they discussed the pros and cons of living in California versus Illinois. Alex studied Judy and Brad's easy banter. He knew Judy had been married and lived in California for as long as he could remember. *Could he wait forty years for Sarah? Yes. But could he bear the pain of Sarah moving on with her life like Judy must have done? No!*

CHAPTER 26

Brad insisted on paying the tab. "It's our treat, Alex. The least we can do for the service and sacrifice you've given.

Alex knew how futile it would be to argue. "Next time, it's on me. You've done a lot yourself, Sir. Judy told me the K9s For Warriors Program was all your idea. What influenced you?"

"My father was a vet, an officer in the Army. Like boys in his generation, he signed up to get away from home. He was a farmer like his dad, and his dad's dad before him. While he was in, his grandfather's death put him in line to run the family farm when he came home. Mom always complained the Army sent the wrong man home. Oh, he ran the farm successfully but he played hard, too. He had adopted the Army's motto: train hard, fight hard and drink hard and that was how he lived."

Alex laughed. "I think every branch of the service has claimed that motto."

Brad nodded and continued. "My dad raised me to walk in his footsteps into the bars and to deal with the lifestyle it incorporates - in and out of jail for drunk and disorderly.

"At the age of sixteen I could work every aspect of the farm and drink and fight just as hard as my old man. After Judy left for California, which was probably good that she did, I used her leaving as an excuse to drink even more. There's a time and a season for everything." He gazed down at Judy. "It was not our time.

"Anyway, when my father died from alcoholism, I realized following in his footsteps, blacking out from drinking, and using the revolving door at the jail, was not how I wanted to live or to die. I got sober. Now forty years later, I got the girl." Brad signed the bill and slid the receipt into his pocket. "I'm going to an AA meeting at the VA in the morning. Why don't you come?"

Alex twisted uncomfortably, as if the question was a gun aimed at his head. Brad jiggled the car keys in his hand, but didn't make a move to get up from the booth.

"I'm not an alcoholic," Alex answered. "I might drink a little too much at times, Sarah thinks I do, but I can quit whenever I want."

"If Sarah wants you to, and you want Sarah, why don't you quit?"

The thought of quitting had never crossed Alex's mind, slowing down maybe, but never quitting. His heart beat quickened at the concept. He gazed around the room and paused on the bar's colorful lights. Patrons sat on stools and more were grouped at the tables. He calculated the time he spent at the Ponderosa, and the money. The issue had been an ongoing argument between him and Sarah.

Brad waited for an answer. Alex looked up and said, "Sure, I'll go. What time?"

"Six-thirty in the morning. I try to catch a meeting before I go down to the precinct. I know it's Sunday, but I always go to the office for a few hours. It's quiet and I get a lot of paperwork done."

First light filtered through the window, warming Alex's cheek as he slept. His eyes sprang open to the faint sound of dogs barking and it took a moment to register his location. Not the FOB, not in his bed with Sarah, and not at Kevin's. He couldn't believe he'd slept at all. His feet hit the floor. He scanned the area for Spider Cat. No cat. He hoped the pesky feline was okay.

In Brad's truck, limited conversation made the short ride to the vet center seem longer. When they arrived, Alex followed Brad inside and, just like the vet center in California, the aroma of coffee primed his secondary addiction - caffeine. A dozen men and women lingered around the room or stood in line at the coffee pot.

"Get yourself a cup of coffee and grab us a couple of seats." Brad left him standing like a teenage boy on a first date. He moved over to the coffee line. A big bulk of a guy in front of him turned around and reached out his hand. "Master Sergeant Mario Ayala, USA. Welcome."

"Lance Corporeal Alex March, USMC."

Mario didn't release Alex's hand but kept shaking it. "Alex March? You're one of the vets getting a service dog, aren't you? I work in the kennel at the K9's For Warriors Program. Congratulations!"

"Thank you, Sir" Mario finally released his hand and Alex shoved it in his pocket.

"You'll be with us for two weeks. I'm staying in the trailer behind the facility...just until the wife and I get back together. Stop by. Have a cup of java. Anytime." Mario turned, poured his coffee, and found a seat.

A gavel pounded and everyone shuffled to their seats. Someone read the Twelve Steps of AA and another read the Twelve Traditions. As the group shared their stories of what it used to be like when they had been drinking, what happened, and what it was like sober, Alex began to identify. He had never really tried to stop drinking but decided now would be a good time. He knew how close his experiences compared to these people. Who knows? Sarah and Kevin might have a warrant out for his arrest right now? And if it weren't for Kevin and his folks he'd probably be sleeping in his truck. Relief washed over him as he realized drinking was a large part of his problems. His drinking affected his marriage, he just hadn't wanted to admit it. He didn't want Aiden to have a drunk for a father, but the thought of not drinking terrified him. *What if he couldn't stop?* He only had to quit one day at a time. That's what Mario said in his drunk-a-log. He'd just quit for today.

Just for today. He could do that. He had already done one day. Loud clapping interrupted his musings and he joined the crowd as they stood up, formed a circle and clasped hands. They recited the serenity prayer, broke the formation, and the room filled with the friendly chatter of camaraderie. He thought of his unit.

CHAPTER 27

When he returned from the AA meeting, Alex showered, dressed, and had a cigarette out on the patio. He studied the morning shadows as they crept inside and faded into the proud Marine Corps colors. He wondered if his life would transform the same way tomorrow when he got his dog. Perhaps his miserable life was about to change, but he didn't dare hope.

He crushed out his cigarette and squeezed the empty pack with his fist. He rose, picked the butt from the ashtray and tossed the remnants of his habit into the waste can. He glanced around the room and, satisfied everything was in order, opened the door. Brad had mentioned there was a small gym and he sought it out. He spent the next forty-five minutes working out, just to keep loose. Finished, he followed the voices coming from down the hall and made his way into the kitchen and dining area.

A plush leather couch, chairs and a long table furnished the dining area. A woman about thirty, with a fire-brick-red French braid that reached down her back, sat at the long oak table. She wore black polyester tear-away pants. A neon-pink stripe traced down her hip, her long leg and draped over the arch of her bare foot. He thought of Sarah. The woman's toes in her sandaled feet wiggled with the same pink shade of nail polish as she talked. Her slim but strong arms waved in some sort of demonstration to the man who sat across from her. Even in the dim morning light, her muscles rippled under her well-oiled and tanned skin. One hand cupped a coffee mug while the bright flamingo tips of her other absently fingered the strap of what appeared to be an expensive camera.

The man sitting across from her wore cammies and a t-shirt. He smiled and nodded when Alex approached the table.

The woman's green eyes scanned over Alex as the man pointed toward the kitchen. "Stick your head around the corner. The gal will pour you some coffee." As he talked, he rose, and with faltering steps moved around the table toward Alex. "I'm Private First Class Steve Pacheco, USA."

Alex eyes frisked the soldier. His t-shirt stretched tight across well-developed biceps. His solid build proved he worked out above and beyond basic PT requirements. The warrior took a step closer and Alex noticed metal extending into the warrior's tennis shoe. Steve wore a prosthesis.

Alex reached out. "Lance Corporal Alex March, USMC." The man steadied himself with his left hand on the table and extended his right to Alex. They shook hands and the soldier motioned to the woman. "This Is Stacey Kraft, USAF." Alex only nodded, then turned and poked his head around the corner into the kitchen. A man at the grill and a woman, whose arms were dusted in flour, looked up.

"Hey, Alex March. Great to see you again." Mario, the veteran from the AA meeting, laid down his spatula, stepped away from the grill and grabbed his hand. "I'm helping Carrie out," he said and turned toward the woman whisking up a huge bowl of pancake batter. "Alex, meet Carrie. She's does a little bit of everything around here. She's a puppy raiser and she's also going to culinary school, a woman of many talents. These blueberry pancakes will melt in your miserable mouth."

"Nice to meet you, Ma'am."

Mario poured coffee into a mug and handed it to Alex. He pointed, "Sugar and cream are over there. Have a seat with the other recruits. Breakfast will be ready in a jiff."

Alex took a seat next to Steve, across from Stacey. Her snug top dipped low enough to reveal the glint of dog tags disappearing into her cleavage. Eyes that sparkled like the mint green surf from back home met his when he pulled them from the crevice.

"Are you nervous about tomorrow?" she asked. "I am. I've never had a dog before. Always wanted one though. I've been reading everything I can about owning a dog. From all I've read it's like having a baby. I helped my sis get ready when she was pregnant with twins. The shopping, decorating the room, the doctor's appointments. So now, I've checked out the veterinarians at home, fenced my yard, and bought out the toy department at Petco. I'm so nervous. "She caught her breath and laughed.

"Not me. I'm pumped." Steve said. "My buddy already has a dog. I've seen what they do."

Alex didn't comment. His buddy had a dog, too. His ex-buddy. He had seen the change in Kevin, but that didn't mean Alex's dog would even like him.

"So where you from, Alex?" Dark, cardinal eyelashes shadowed those sea-green eyes.

"California." He eyed the camera beside her.

"That was my job," she said. "Combat photographer." Her smile gentled her face. Age had begun to characterize her features with lines that captioned her lips like a parenthesis.

He didn't look away. "How about you? Where do you put down your boots? "He asked, wondering why she was here. She seemed normal. *Did she sleep through the night?*

"Charleston. Born and raised."

"Here you go, folks." Mario and Carrie entered the dining area, hefting two steaming platters. The savory aroma reached Alex's nose before

Mario and Carrie placed the feast on the table. "Sausage and bacon," Carrie announced as she set the platter down. The links still sizzled. "This is not Jimmy Dean store bought fixins." Carrie went on. "It's been donated by a local butcher who cures and seasons fresh cut, local farm raised pork to perfection. He's fed two presidents and countless heads of states. When he heard about your arrival, he wanted to do his part. You won't taste anything better."

Mario set the tray he carried next to the meat platter. "I told you, this gal can cook. Fresh blueberry pancakes. Wait til you taste these." Melted butter dripped slowly down over the flapjacks' edges and puddled onto the plate.

The firehouse redhead, he couldn't remember her name, thrust her fork into a sausage and bit into the link. Alex's stomach growled, flip-flopped, and his loins stirred. Now he looked away, squirmed and dragged his attention back to the last two platters, one heaped with eggs, scrambled or sunny side up, and toast, and the other, a colorful array of fruit. He still felt the stirrings, and then blushed, when he realized it was only the vibration of his cell.

He pulled the phone from his pocket. Aiden's face beamed up at him. Guilt killed any action below the belt. He hit the decline button and laid the device on the table. He kept his head down and stabbed a couple slices of bacon.

"Was that a picture of your son?" Steve aimed his fork at the phone.

Alex shoveled scrambled eggs onto his plate. "Yeah." His face burned with embarrassment as if the two had read his mind.

"How old is he?" Steve asked. The redhead didn't care.

"Almost a year and a half. Aiden. His name's Aiden."

"My nephew's two. You'll have your hands full when he hits two. At that age they can bring a hard ass drill sergeant to his knees with tears of frustration."

"We're separated." He felt those mint-green eyes on him.

"Hey, I'm sorry man. Do you think you'll get it back?"

"I don't know. It doesn't look good."

"Well don't give up the fight. The buddy I told you about? The one with the service dog? Everything changed after he got his dog, Tank. His story's like a fairy tale."

Alex nodded and scraped his plate clean with the last bite of toast. He had given up on fairy tales a long time ago. He started to get up when the redhead touched his arm. "We're going to the Cozy Dog for lunch and then hitting some of the other tourist stops, you know Lincoln's Home, Lincoln's Tomb. You in?"

His arm was on fire. "I don't know. I'll see."

CHAPTER 28

Alex headed out the back door and found the path that led around the perimeter encompassing the five acres of the K9s for Warriors. Brad had told him he ran the five mile track every morning after he used the workout room. Alex began a slow jog with the redhead on his mind and Aiden's image in his pocket. Anger pushed up his pace and he concentrated on the landscape. Barren buzz-cut cornfields reminded him of his first Marine Corps haircut. Two rabbits hopped across the stubble and disappeared. He approached a grove of apple and peach trees at the rear of the property and wondered if Brad's mom had once made apple pies and peach jam. According to Brad, although this picturesque setting portrayed the American dream, the Chief had dealt with his own demons.

That's the trouble with Americans, Alex thought, as his boots beat along the path, we have life easy. For most of us, meals and safety are not an issue, so we expect so much more. People living in war torn countries, who have to fight for every bit of food and security, there are no options.

The warrior pushed on under the coolness of the trees' canopy. His legs burned and his hot breath vaporized into steady puffs before him. A plane buzzed overhead and he resisted the urge to hit the ground. The sun's rays blinded him as he emerged from the grove. Sweat trickled down his temples and back. His heart pumped steady.

He ran harder, taking it to his limit and then pushed beyond. In this zone the good images came. Sarah and Aiden, laughing and rolling around on the floor as she raised the little guy up over her prone body while the boy giggled and kicked. "Aiden, you're flying!" she'd say. The good times.

Spent, he returned to his room and stripped again. He stepped under the shower's cold spray and let the icicled daggers pelt his back, distracting his mind from erotic memories of showers with Sarah.

Dressed, he lay down on the bed and steeled himself to check his emails and texts. A long email from Sarah. "I'm sorry for the things I said. I didn't mean it….Please, let's talk. We have to talk…. I understand why you did what you did… but it's not what it looked like. I love YOU, Alex. There will never be anyone else." Then the guilt. "Aiden misses you. I need you."

He read on. "I thought you shipped out without saying good bye. I talked to Judy, I'm so glad you are getting a dog. Please come home."

Kevin's attempt at repairing the relationship was a text. "Get your head out of your ass, Jarhead. Call me."

He laid the phone on the bedside table. How many beers would he have had by now? He picked up the brochure from the AA meeting. There was another meeting at eight tonight. He'd check with Mario, maybe get a lift.

The knock on his door woke him. He couldn't believe he'd dozed off. The redhead wore the same sweats, they hung loose on her hips. A hot pink string necklace laced through pale chunks of quartz and matched dangling earrings. The jewelry did not distract him from seeking her dog tags that still remained in their warm, covert position.

"Time to move out, Marine, if you're going." She smiled again, and her gaze slid over his body.

He grabbed his jacket and phone. Before she could enter the room, he edged her out of the way, and stepped into the hall, closing the door behind them.

"Mario's driving us." He felt her eyes on his rear as she let Alex stride ahead.

At the Cozy Dog Drive-In, Mario explained the restaurant's history while Stacey snapped photos.

"Two guys, Ed and Dan, invented the deep-fried, battered hot dogs while they were stationed in Amarillo, Texas during World War II. They served them at the USO and the base PX and called them Crusty Curs. When Ed came home, his wife suggested the name wasn't appropriate for the civilian customers so they renamed them Cozy Dogs. In 1946 they became a hit when he began selling them at the Illinois State fair." Mario stood back, pointed toward the cardboard cut-out of two, embracing Cozy Dogs and said, "And that's the story of the birth of the corn dog, my friends, right here on Route 66."

While they waited for their food, Stacey wanted Mario to take a picture with the three of them gathered around the six foot cardboard cut-out of the two loving Cozy Dogs. "You know you three are the first vets to receive dogs from the K9s For Warriors?" Mario said, "So we're all making history, too."

As they ate, Alex wondered if there was anything the redhead could do that would not make his pulse throb. He knew he could have her. She constantly touched his arm and batted her eyes. To counter, he kept his conversation limited to Steve and Mario. Mario's whirlwind tour of the city returned them to the facility in time for steak dinner, again, from the local butcher. Baked potatoes, beans and home-made bread finished off the menu.

Mario came out from the kitchen as the trio swiped their dessert plates clean and said, "I'll come by your room after I finish with feeding the dogs and cleaning the kennels." He gathered Stacey's and Steve's plates and asked, "How about you two? An AA meeting to fine tune your treatment program?"

Stacey nodded. "I'll tag along. Not much to do here."

Great. Alex groaned as he took the last bite of pie. Stacey and Steve looked over at him. He glanced up, pointed to his dessert. "The pie. It's so good."

At the AA meeting, Stacey followed in his shadow like a new recruit, sitting next to him and hanging with him during the break. He thought she might just be nervous about tomorrow, he knew his nerves were keyed. Two days without alcohol. He'd never sleep.

When they returned from the meeting, Mario parked the facility's van in its reserved spot. "Tomorrow's the big day. See you guys at the orientation." He disappeared around the back of the building to his trailer. Alex hesitated, afraid to head for his room. I think I'll catch some TV. I'm not going to be able to sleep."

"Me too," she said.

In the rec room, he grabbed the remote, flopped back onto the leather couch and began flipping through channels. He kept his eyes on the screen as the female warrior's body settled in next to his.

Heat raced up his thighs, his arms, to his head, yet he didn't move. He felt stuck deep in the folds of the couch like the Hummer when it hit a dune and became buried to its chassis. He smelled her. He felt her body heat. He shouldn't have turned his head but he did. Siren's eyes in a deep emerald sea met his. He couldn't breathe.

CHAPTER 29

"Okay everyone." Judy met each vet's eyes as they sat before her. "You will be receiving orientation packets after you're paired up with your service dog." She held up a bulging, blue tote imprinted with the K-9 For Warriors logo. "The packet contains your dog's medical history and the contact information of its puppy raiser, in case you have any questions about your dog's training or history. We included grooming items, a sample of your dog's favorite treat, such as a favorite toy or chew bone, and my favorite, a puppy album." She held up an album. "We tried to capture the cutest and proudest moments during the past twenty months." She smiled at each veteran. "Do you have any questions?"

The group exchanged blank stares, but their brows creased with worry. Judy smiled again, and they turned to one another. Now, their expressions ran the gamut of emotions. Steve's raised eyebrows creased his forehead and his jaw muscles flexed, yet he grinned in anticipation. Stacey's face lined with worry, as if she might cry. Alex sat expressionless and clamped his mouth pencil-thin. Exchanging anxious looks, they nodded their heads in unison. "We're ready."

"Good. We'll be bringing out the dogs in a minute."

Brad entered through a door at the corner of the long room. Soft murmurs amongst the vets amplified the tension. Brad led two of the dogs, while Carrie led a third. They stopped at the far end. Brad handed over a leash to Judy which Alex assumed was Masada's. He figured each dog took a position beside the person who had nurtured and trained it for the first year of its life. There had been four puppies in the litter, but Judy had mentioned one puppy had not made the cut as a service dog. The tension in the room was thick. This was it. Judy nodded and Carrie and Brad reached down and removed the dogs' leads.

Judy patted Masada and said, "Greet!"

Brad and Carrie echoed the command, and their dogs bolted across the room. But Masada did not respond and instead, remained at Judy's side. She hung back, studying the scene before her. Was she going to pick a veteran? Was she allowing her littermates to choose, and she would pick who was left?

Alex guessed the larger dog was the male named Rocky, followed the smaller female dog, Daisy, as she greeted each warrior. It seemed the female instructed her littermate as what to do. "First you greet everyone, make them feel comfortable." Daisy glanced back at Rocky, making sure he followed her lead. What did she say then? "You take Steve and I'll take the woman?" Because that's what happened.

After Daisy greeted Steve, Stacey and finally Alex, with Rocky tailing behind, then, as if completing her social obligations, she turned back to Stacey, and laid her head on her knee.

Stacey melted. Sliding off her chair to the floor, she wrapped her arms around Daisy and buried her face in the service dog's fur. When she straightened, she held Daisy's head and kissed her damp, black nose. Peering over the dog's back, she read the name on the vest. "Daisy? Is that your name, girl?" The tears streamed down the warrior's face unguarded. She pulled Daisy's face to hers and kissed her, over again and over again. "My new team mate."

Rocky left Daisy with Stacey, and nuzzled up to Steve. The dog rested his head on the warrior's knee. "Hey, Rocky. It's you and me boy." Steve, too, caved to a flood of emotions, fell to his knees and hugged his dog.

Alex's heart sank, and panic begin to throb in his temples. No dog had picked him. Masada remained beside Judy. Alex dared to look at the dog who he believed shunned him. Masada's eyes met his. As if in slow motion, Masada stood, and floated across the room toward Alex. He heard Judy inhale and exhale in exaggerated sobs, her tears glistened on her face. Masada reached Alex, sat down, and faced him. Masada's twenty month journey was over. Alex wanted to cry, but still a Marine, he focused on the mission. He dropped to his knees. Masada laid her head on his thigh and rolled her eyes up at his. He cupped her head in his hands, leaned down, and kissed the top of her head.

And, as quickly as that, it was done. The bond was sealed. He knew he would take a bullet for this dog, and he knew she would do the same for him.

Alex had just witnessed the final chapter in Masada's journey. Judy had explained she believed a dog possessed its own acumen, or sixth sense as whom to choose as a teammate. "The dog knows," she'd said. Alex squeezed his eyes closed to dam the rising flood behind them, and pressed his lips together to restrain the roar yearning to burst from his lungs.

Ooh rah.

CHAPTER 30

Alex woke from a fitful sleep before the sun lit up his small patio. Since he had returned from Iraq he hated the shades of grey in the long night, yet loved the solitude. He coveted being alone, but yearned for the company of his family. In the grey dawn he dreamed of relishing the rush of adrenaline in his veins, but lusted equally for the release of his desires with Sarah. Irritated, he jumped from the bed and stumbled, almost stepping on Masada.

He bent down, cupped her head and scratched her ears. "Sorry Masada." How could he have forgotten? The dog had helped him through the night, waking him repeatedly, like Stacey had described. His mood lightened. "Do you want to go for a run, girl?" He didn't have to dress because, even after all this time, he still slept in sweats and his boots.

He buckled Masada into her service vest and sought out the gym. After thirty minutes of warm up exercises, Alex regarded Masada as she lay waiting. "Okay, girl, now let's go for a run. I'll bet you'll like that." The thought of the dog running alongside thrilled him. He passed the full length mirror beside the door and the image grinning back appeared as a stranger who had no sense.

Unleashed, Masada ran by his side for the first mile. She sensed the purpose of the run and burst forward effortlessly. She stretched out and thundered down the path ahead. Alex's heart lurched, sending a shock of panic through him as his dog galloped away. His pace faltered just as she stopped and turned around. Was she laughing at him? She waited for him to catch up, and then bounded ahead again. When he moved through the grove of fruit trees, she dropped back and matched his pace, as if sensing his high alert as he scanned the branches and occasional bush. Once out of the grove, she, again, left him in her dust, only to stop ahead and goad him on, like his old drill sergeant.

Back in his room Alex showered and shaved while Masada crunched her kibble and lapped water. He stepped out of the bathroom and found his service dog sitting at attention. She reminded him of a recruit addressing a superior if it had not been for the pink rabbit that bulged from her mouth. Her lips splayed out and draped over the pink fluffy form. Her alert ears spread apart and folded against her head. She rolled her eyes up at him and deposited the bunny at his feet.

Alex snatched up the soggy rabbit and tossed it while he toweled off and dressed quickly. The knowledge of the day's agenda wadded his stomach into tangles. A trip to the mall. He had only been to the mall once since returning from Iraq. He had accompanied Sarah and Aiden to Babies R Us. The clatter of the shops' iron gates rolling open added to his already unexplained and unbearable stress. As more and more people filled the mall, anger overrode his fear, confusion and embarrassment. The echoing voices, yelling and laughter seemed to gang up, inducing him to sweat profusely. The day concluded when he could take no more. He dragged Sarah and Aiden back to the truck and never went to the mall again. But then, Sarah never invited him again.

"Everyone's awfully quiet. Did I miss something?" Alex asked as he sat down at the long, oak dining table. Stacey and Steve sat across from one another, doctoring their breakfasts with salt, pepper and hot sauce.

Pausing, they made eye contact with each other, and Steve answered. "I'm not excited about going to the mall." He turned to Stacey.

"Me either," Stacey said. The sea green eyes swept over Alex like a rip tide. "How about you?"

"It's supposed to be better with the dogs, but I don't see how," Alex answered.

He couldn't draw his eyes from hers. Steve and Stacy nodded and returned to their breakfast.

The Illinois malls were no different than California's. The instructions for handling the dogs as they entered and exited the van still swam in Alex's head as the dogs calmly awaited for the mall's sliding doors to open. Lunch hour herded the crowds toward the food court and the three teams, with Judy and Carrie hovering behind, joined the movement.

The group passed a couple standing at a shop window with two children. Catching sight of the dogs, the family turned and approached Alex and Masada. Alarm bells sounded in Alex's head and his heartbeat quickened. With an agility that startled Alex, Masada stepped in front of him and blocked the couple and their children from coming any closer to her charge. Although Masada's action surprised Alex, her calmness assured him and he decided there was no need to panic. It was just an ordinary American family. The woman was asking a question.

"Can we pet him?" she said. Alex's eyes flashed to Judy, who shook her head and mouthed, "No."

He turned back to the couple and remembered the response Judy had taught during orientation. "No, I'm sorry. She's a service dog. She's working."

The father frowned, but his wife said, "Oh, I've heard about these dogs." She questioned her partner. "You remember, don't you, Tim? On 60 Minutes?" Tim nodded and she turned back to Alex. "Are you a veteran?"

"Yes ma'am."

"Well, I want to thank you for your service and your sacrifice. 60 Minutes made me appreciate what you men and women go through." She peered up at Stacey and Steve who both stood several inches taller than the short woman. "Thank you all," she repeated." And my family thanks you, too." She bent down to her children, five year old twins, Alex guessed, and said, "These people watch over us and keep us safe. You know, like God watches over you, too."

The boy and girl hung behind their parents, but rolled their eyes up at the group and nodded. "Tell them thank you," their father ordered.

Little fingers clung to their mother's and they whispered timidly to the people whom their mother had just compared to God. "Thank you."

Alex knelt down to their level and reached out his hand. He smiled, and grasping her little fingers, shook her tiny hand gently. "You are welcome." Then, switching to a serious expression, Alex faced the boy and shook his soft small hand, and repeated, "You are very welcome."

Alex stood. The parents beamed with pride. He reached out to the couple and shook hands first with the man, "It was nice to meet you, Sir." And then the woman. "Nice to meet you, ma'am."

They continued on to the food court with Judy and Carrie trailing behind, guarding their charges to insure no one tried to feed the dogs and that the vets handled the situation properly if someone did try.

Throughout the day, the noise, chatter and crowds tried Alex's nerves. When he felt over-whelmed, he glanced down and monitored Masada. Each time he saw her calmness. The dog meant everything to him already. He would no longer have to hide in the house or pay the emotional price when he went out.

CHAPTER 31

The first week passed into the second, and the path around the perimeter of Brad's farm became beaten down by, not only Brad, Alex and Masada but now Stacey and Steve also frequented the trail, along with Daisy and Rocky. The dogs loved the run, nipping at each other's heels and ears like they had as puppies.

Steve kept a measured pace next to Alex. "Are you ready to graduate?" Steve asked. Their breaths pumped out rhythmical puffs.

"Man, I don't know. So much is riding on us, our performance, and the dogs' – a lot of pressure, a lot of expectations. I feel like I'm in boot camp all over again… and that's just the graduation." Alex picked up the pace to match the rise of anxiety at the thought.

"What happens when you get home? Did you patch it up with the wife?"

"No. Haven't even called her. I was going to, but then I got the dog. I've used the excuse I've been too busy – and then there's the time difference." Alex's and Steve's boots pounded the path as one. The exaggerated beat muffled Stacey's lighter footfall coming up behind. "Sarah quit leaving texts and voice mails. Like I said, I don't think it's going to work out. How about you? What happens when you get home?"

"My family's military. They're behind me one hundred percent. They weren't at first. My dad and uncles are old guarde. Their motto is, 'Suck it up and move on.' It sounds gruesome, but losing a leg helped them to accept my PTSD. I still think they look at someone like you and Stacey, you know, since your injuries are invisible, and think of you as weak. But people are coming around and attitudes are changing. Even my dad is going to go to treatment with me when I get home."

"You got a girl back home?"

"I did. I proposed to her before I shipped out, but she said everything was moving too fast. Six months into my tour she decided being a military wife wasn't her cup of tea, and she broke it off."

"Sorry, man. That's rough. I would have fallen apart if Sarah had done that to me. She and Aiden were why I signed up. Thinking of them carried me through every firefight."

"Yeah, well, I'm good. The director at the vet center set me up for a bunch of speaking engagements when I return. You know, to help bring awareness about PTSD and the benefits of a service dog. Anyway, I still don't sleep well and with the headaches and anger, I don't think a woman could handle all my problems."

"I feel the same way. I don't want to burden Sarah, she's so young and innocent. I don't want to ruin her and Aiden's lives and, yeah, my counselor at the vet center wants me to do the speaking thing, too. It'll keep me busy."

They rounded the last corner, slowing their pace for the cool down.

"You'll be fine." Steve said. "You and Sarah will work it out."

"We'll see."

Stacey came up from behind and sprinted past. "Sarah would be a fool if she doesn't take him back. Come on, Daisy!"

Back in his room, Alex removed Masada's vest and stripped down for a shower. Vulnerability still prevented Alex from indulging under the hot jets. When he exited the bathroom he discovered Masada, again, waiting, her pink bunny bulged from her mouth and her lips splayed over its fuzzy body. Alex laughed out loud, grabbed the toy, and tossed the stuffed animal for Masada to retrieve. As he dressed she repeatedly dropped her treasure at his feet and he threw it again.

Life is simple here. He wanted to stay forever – in this room with these people who understood him. But he would go home, only this time he would not be alone. He had a team mate.

Sarah. He had to call her. He checked his watch. Eight A.M., six in California, an hour before she left for the salon. He snatched the cell from the table and jabbed the numbers on the screen.

"Hello Alex." Her soft violin voice played like an orchestra. "Hello?" she repeated.

Alex inhaled quickly. "Sarah. Please. I'm sorry, Sarah. I…"

"It's okay Alex. It's going to be okay. I love you. I want to be there for you. I'm begging you, don't shut me out." Her voice was strong, but threaded with pain and desperation." Please Alex. Please don't shut me out."

She was begging him? After what he had done? Shame and guilt wracked his voice up an octave higher and he slumped over the table. "Oh Sarah, I won't. Never again. Everything's going to be okay." Did he actually believe the words he spoke? He looked down at Masada.

"I'm coming to the graduation," she said firmly. He pictured her standing straight backed, at her full height of five foot four inches. He thought of her mother. "I don't care what you think. I'm coming. Kevin said I should not miss it. He said that it will be an important day to remember."

"I would like you to be here, Honey. I do. But I don't have the money for a ticket. The Veterans Center only paid for mine. I'm sorry."

"It's okay, Alex. Everyone here is pitching in. Mom and Dad and Kevin, even your counselor, Mark. They're all behind you one hundred percent. Even some of my customers are tipping more than usual for the cause. So, I'll be there. I want to meet your dog. What's its name?"

"Her name's Masada. Oh she's wonderful, Sarah. And she's beautiful too. You'll love her. Aiden will love her, too. But she's a working dog so we can't treat her like a pet. Oh, she plays too, it's not like she doesn't act like a dog. When she doesn't have her vest on she's just like a regular dog. Well, she is a dog. You know what I mean." Alex stopped to catch his breath. Tears rolled freely down his face and he tasted the salt on his lips as he described his service dog that was changing his life.

"She sounds wonderful, Alex. Send a photo."

"I'll pick you up at the airport," he said. "We'll pick you up. Me and Masada."

CHAPTER 32

The last days at K9s For Warriors were full. Excursions to the mall, noisy restaurants and the busy Capitol Airport were just a few of the last field trips squeezed into the schedule to insure the veterans could handle the dogs and remain calm among crowds and in stressful, unexpected situations. The limited time whizzed by, bringing graduation and reality closer and closer. It was now Sunday, the day before graduation. October carried an occasional icy northern blast which promised more to come in the months ahead.

Today, the schedule offered a break of free time in the morning before their trip to the prison at one. "It's a time to catch your breath, enjoy the outdoors," Judy had said when she and Brad invited Alex to accompany them to collect black walnuts out by the lake.

Alex figured Masada would enjoy the outing. They parked alongside the dirt road and Brad and Judy grabbed gunny sacks from the trunk.

"Have you ever done this before?" Brad asked. Alex admitted he had not. He followed Judy and

Brad as they hiked down a path toward the walnut groves that sheltered the lake's bank.

Enjoying the outdoors, Alex slapped the unattached lead against his leg, and kept his eyes on Masada as she loped ahead, sniffing every branch and bush. He smiled when she jumped into the air and took chase after a jack rabbit bolting from the scrub. He allowed her the thrill of the chase until she disappeared into a thicket, and then shouted, "Masada come!" She obeyed like a new recruit in boot camp, did an about face, and came bounding back toward him.

"Good girl!" Alex laughed as Masada jumped up and danced before him, and then bounded away, enjoying her freedom and chasing the autumn leaves blowing across the path.

Judy turned to Alex and asked. "Have the days flown by for you?"

"I can't believe what's happening," Alex held a broken branch and dragged it along the ground making designs in the dirt. "It's only been two weeks, but when we go to the mall or crowded places where I used to get anxious, and I still do, I look down at Masada and see she's calm, that's all I need. If she's calm, everything's okay, and if anyone gets too close, she steps between me and them. They're usually only interested in her anyway. I can't wait to take her with me to my classes. It's going to be so different."

"How are you sleeping?" Brad asked.

Alex hit the branch against a rotting stump. "I still don't sleep through the night. I'm always waking up, but it's because Masada wakes me when the nightmares come. It's incredible. No one could have made me believe how a service dog can change your life." He studied a raccoon on the far bank. It busied itself with something cradled in its paws, dunking it in the water, pulling it out, and examining it. "Did I tell you Sarah's coming to graduation?"

"Really? That's great Alex. She had called me, so worried about you. I'm glad you two are working it out." Judy said as she gathered up the walnuts scattered under a tree while Brad held open the gunny sack.

"Maybe it will be okay. Maybe." Alex, again, whacked at the stick against the tree stump.

"I hear Stacey's daughter is flying in, too," Judy added as she stood up. "The graduation is going to be a great occasion."

Brad twisted and knotted the bumpy, bulging bag. "When is Sarah getting in?"

"Oh eight hundred tomorrow."

"You can take the van and pick her up."

"Thank you, sir, but I was going to rent a car."

Brad slung the sack of walnuts over his shoulder. . "I insist. It's part of the perks."

They spent the rest of the morning kicking through the fallen leaves, breathing the musky air, and scouring the forest floor for every last walnut. "These are going to make the best cookies," Judy said as she loaded her sack into the van. "I'll make some for you and Sarah to take home," Judy said. "You guys will love them. Black walnuts are hard to find in California. That way you won't forget us a couple of months from now when you are enjoying eighty degree weather and we're here freezing our butts off in an Illinois blizzard."

Alex lifted his sack into the van. "I'll never forget you and what you have done. And thank you for this morning. It has been great to get away."

They arrived back at the facility early enough for Alex to stretch out on the bed and relax. He scanned his room in the soft filtered light and knew he would never forget this place. He wanted to tell the whole world about his experience here. He wanted to stay here in this warm cocoon of understanding and support, yet he wanted to go home to everything familiar. His roots. He could hardly wait to finish school. Provide for his family, be honorable again. And he wanted to take Aiden to Disneyland, to the beach, and to pick him up from school. He wanted everything.

At one o'clock Judy, Brad, Carrie and the veterans with their dogs, all loaded into the van to make their last field trip before graduation, the trip to the prison to meet the volunteer inmates who had played such a significant part in the training of their service dogs. As they climbed into the van, Judy said, "Meeting the inmates will give you the opportunity to thank them, and in turn, the inmates will meet you guys and realize the magnitude of their efforts."

The guards waved the van through the gate. The Prison loomed ahead as Brad eased the vehicle toward the unloading area. Alex shuddered as the gate's iron bars scraped and clanged across the only exit. From the back window, he peered up at the thick, formable concrete walls topped with barbed wire and sectioned off by strategically positioned guard towers. Just like the FOB.

He turned away from the oddly familiar surroundings and stared ahead. His knee jerked up and down while his thoughts soared over the walls. Visions of his life panned in a panoramic review of conflicting clips about war and survival. Too much to absorb. The firefights and erotic nights with Sarah, nightmares and watching his son sleep, holding Sarah and cradling a fallen comrade. Too much.

The guards herded the group to a specially assigned visitor's area reserved for the veterans and their dogs. The three teams, Alex and Masada, Steve and Rocky, and Stacey and Daisy followed by Brad, Judy, and finally, Carrie, who led a fourth dog named, Boise, all lined up against the wall.

They focused on the side door that led into the prison.

A guard stood at attention at the door and three additional sentries were posted at each corner of the room. A knock on the door alerted them. The guard by the door tensed and made eye contact with his team. He nodded to each of the other officers. Satisfied, he turned, lifted the latch, and opened the door. Chains clanked against the institutional green linoleum, followed by six inmates in orange jumpsuits filing into the room. They shuffled in, their ankles clad in blue iron shackles, elbows straight, their hands, clasped in front, and restrained by cuffs. The prisoners lined up and faced their visitors. Grim stares and silence made the gap seemed wider than it was between the two groups.

Brad's slight nod stirred up a rustle of crisp uniforms as the guards moved from their posts and approached the inmates. The prisoners offered up their wrists and key rings rattled, adding to the quiet, as an officer turned the locks on the cuffs and another stooped down to do the same for the shackles. Appreciating the false freedom, the men rubbed their wrists, but remained tense and rooted as they stared ahead without making eye contact with the veterans standing before them.

Masada, Rocky, Daisy, and even Boise, sat poised, ears and eyes on the line of men before them. The guards returned to their posts.

A small whine caused the dozen heads to turn down and focus on the source. Masada sat beside Alex, shifting from one paw to the other. She whined again, another whine, this time from Rocky, and then, Boise joined in. On cue, as a unit, the veterans knelt down, unsnapped their dogs' leads and ordered, "Greet!"

The room came alive as the inmates knelt down, and the dogs bounded forward, jumping into the prisoners' open arms. The space that had seemed so vast, between the two groups, now danced with wagging tails, laughter and tearful greetings of "Hey, how are you?", "Good dog," and, "I missed you."

Alex was the first to follow his dog across the gap of swinging tails and wiggling butts. He crouched down beside Masada and Roy and introduced himself. "I want to thank you for what you have done," he said to Roy. "Masada is an amazing dog. In just these two weeks she has changed my life." Alex's vision blurred, like it did every time he talked about Masada, or even thought about what she meant to him.

Roy looked up at him with his own watery eyes. "Thank you. I enjoyed every minute. She has changed my life, too." He patted Masada as he spoke. "It has been an honor to be a part of this program, and as an American, I want to thank you for your sacrifice and contribution to our country's freedom. I hope you will be able to enjoy your freedom, and live a better life with Masada." He reached over Masada and shook Alex's hand. The hands of the two wounded men held a few moments longer, each feeling the significance of what they had become, because of the dog between them.

The hour passed quickly with the inmates and veterans exchanging dog stories, laughs, fist pounds and high fives. Brad, Judy and Carrie stood back, moved by what they had accomplished. After a discreet nod from Brad, the guards signaled the inmates who stood and gave their final hugs and handshakes.

Alex regarded the inmates as they were, once again, shackled and cuffed. They marched back into the bowels of the prison, this time with shoulders straighter, chests swelled out and eyes brighter. Alex hoped their experience with the dogs allowed them to see past the concrete walls and someday make it back under the wire.

CHAPTER 33

From a dead sleep, Alex's eyes sprang open. He killed the insistent buzz of his cell phone's alarm. Masada's warmth stretched the length of his body. Awake too, she lifted her head and studied her warrior lying beside her. He filled in the words she was unable to say, "Good morning, jarhead." He tousled the fur between her ears. A warmth swelled inside of him when her sable eyes softened and absorbed his caresses.

"We're burning daylight." Alex said, gently jostling the dog. "Down, Girl. It's a big day. You meet Sarah today." She jumped from the bed and he threw back the covers. He began to rise, but paused. When was the last time he greeted the morning with such enthusiasm and absence of dread? For that matter, when had the dawn ever slipped past him leaving the alarm to wake him? When had he not laid in bed waiting for the morning greys to creep into the room and taunt him about the coming day's stark reality?

Masada lapped water from her bowl, then sniffed her empty food bowl, and looked back at him. "I've got you covered," he said and jumped up from the bed. He crossed the room and snatched up her bag of food. She danced a two-step as the kibble tinkled into her steel bowl. "There you go, girl."

In the bathroom he splashed water on his face and slapped on his cap. "Save some kibble for later. Time for PT." Masada eagerly abandoned her breakfast when Alex grabbed her leash. "I know. You love PT."

A foreign lightness flowed in his veins while his boots beat their steady rhythm on the well-worn path. He loved PT, too. His thoughts floated like the white clouds after a dark rainy day. He felt as if he could fly. Masada ran easily beside him. Her ears lay back, close to her head, tail low and billowing. Her eyes squinted from the wind in her face and her coat rippled in the golden morning sun. Only two weeks, yet he felt like he'd had Masada for a lifetime

He realized the trips to the mall, the crowded restaurants, and the noisy airport, had become almost routine. His breath pumped in and out as he ran, strong and steady. His mind, too, felt strong and steady, but still he continued his internal argument. How had it happened? How had the dog accomplished so much? It had only been two weeks. .

The man and dog rounded the corner. Masada ran flat out, a hundred yards ahead, her chest low to the ground, her nose reached out like a thoroughbred approaching the finish line. She would disappear into the groves, if she continued, but, as always, she slowed, turned around, and taunted him. Again, Alex imagined the words she couldn't speak. "Come on, recruit! You run like a little girl!"

They finished their run, Masada her breakfast, and Alex his shower. He tossed her bunny as he dressed, made the bed, and stepped out on the patio for a smoke. He thought about quitting the cigarettes, too, but in AA they advised, "Tackle one addiction at a time." Maybe after his first year of sobriety. He tallied up the days without a drink, sixteen days. Unbelievable. Sarah won't believe it. He didn't believe it.

He closed the door to his room quietly. No time for his breakfast, and with Masada trotting beside him, Alex made his way out to Mario's trailer and tapped on the door. Like the big ogre, Shrek, dressed in Army green sweats, Mario filled the doorway. "Morning. You here for the key?"

"Yes, thanks. I'm running late. Can't believe it, I almost overslept."

Mario handed him the van's keys. "You've got my number. Any problems, call me. See you at the graduation. You can give back the keys then."

"You got it." Alex gave Mario a quick fist pound and he and Masada sprinted to the parking lot. Unlocking the van, he ordered, "Up," and Masada sprang into the passenger seat. "Good girl." He hustled in after her and fired up the engine.

His heart rate increased along with the traffic as they neared the airport. With his arm, he swiped at the trickling beads of perspiration threatening to soak his shirt. His fingers clamped the wheel and he focused on the roadside, scanning for debris. He steered into the freeway's slow lane to make the airport exit. A Starbuck's paper cup, tossed from the car in front of him, rolled across his lane. He swerved to avoid it just as the Prius in the next lane screeched its brakes and blared its little eco-green horn. Red lights flashed ahead and Alex stomped on his brakes. His head pounded like war drums.

Masada dug her nails into the seat and braced against the thrust. Alex glanced at his precious, priceless cargo and immediately reined in his racing brain. He berated himself. Masada's presence ranked on the same life-saving level of importance as his M16, his Kevlar jacket, and his helmet. The dog was all that gear wrapped in one soft golden package with a black shiny nose and pink tongue. "Sorry Masada. I'll take it down a notch."

The remainder of the trip passed uneventfully. He parked and, with Masada trotting alongside, he entered the terminal. Inside he scanned the display of flight schedules as a security guard approached, one hand resting on the handle of a billy club bobbing from his belt. "Sorry, sir. No dogs allowed in the terminal. You'll have to step outside."

Alex pointed to Masada's vest. "She's a service dog."

The guard fingered his club while he studied the vest. "I'm sorry sir. Do you have any identification? We allow only certified service dogs."

Alex remembered the ID card Judy had issued the first day. "Yes sir. It's here. In my pocket." He fished out the laminated card from his wallet.

The guard's peach-fuzz face squashed any attempt at intimidation. Youth delayed any chance of filling out the uniform. His shirt bloused at his shoulders, while the dark blue material gathered in pleats at his waist and disappeared under his tightly drawn belt. If Alex grabbed the strap and yanked the leather strap loose, the boy's pants would drop to the floor. He handed the ID to the kid. "There you go."

The fuzz face frowned, examined it, and flipped the card over a couple of times. He eyed Alex and handed it back. "Thank you, sir. Sorry for the delay. Are you picking someone up?"

"Yes, my wife. She's flying in from California, well from Chicago, she had a layover in Chicago."

"Go to the baggage area at the east end." He pointed. "By the door with the letter D. See it? You can't go to the gate without a ticket. Your wife's flight's on time."

"Thank you, sir." Alex returned the ID to the wallet, thankful the kid didn't turn the ordeal into an inquisition. Judy had warned everyone during orientation that, many times, airline, hotel and restaurant personnel think they are justified in asking the nature of the disability and what purpose the dog serves, especially when the disability is not apparent. An interrogation forcing him to air his problems, especially to some punk kid, would have angered him.

The baggage carousel rotated slowly. Each turn, took on another bag or two. Alex's stomach fluttered now that he was here, waiting. He hadn't thought of what he would say. What should he say? Should he grab her and hug her? How was your flight, seemed lame. Masada pushed her nose against his hand. He looked down and those deep sable eyes stared up at him. She nudged him again. His tension eased and he squatted, resting his arm on her back. Passengers, laboring with their carry-ons, began to filter into the baggage claim area. The travelers lit up in recognition to occasional shouts of greetings from the awaiting crowd.

Perhaps, because the separation had seemed like a lifetime, Alex paused and held his breath before he shouted his greeting. The woman he recognized wore a blue blazer over a button down shirt and black dress slacks. Nice shoes, no sneakers. Not her favorite lace crop top. No harem pants or skinny jeans. This woman scanned the area and locked eyes with her Marine.

Alex stared. She smiled. His heart squeezed inside his chest and he thought he heard himself whimper from passionate anguish at the sight of her. She licked her lips. He tried to pull his tongue from the dry roof of his mouth. He couldn't call out because he couldn't speak. The woman walked toward him with the confidence of a model on a runway. He remained in place and stared. She had not packed her silly girlish notions or her mothering attitude. She was all business. Her emerald green eyes were on fire, and, this time, he knew he heard himself moan. She stopped in front of him.

The airport noises faded. This girl he had left in California could easily bring him to his knees with her innocence. But this was not a girl, this was a no-nonsense woman standing before him. Funny he had not noticed the transformation before. In Iraq, in the middle of a firefight, he had always been in complete control, even when he didn't know if he would survive through the next round of hammering bullets, but now, this woman before him, as her deep green eyes stung his senses, promised him more than he ever imagined. She could be the devil in disguise, yet he would do anything for her.

He took her hand, pulled her close, and embraced her. She still smelled of strawberries.

They exchanged no words and reserved their passionate kisses for later. Instead, Alex sensed a mysterious confidence between them that everything was going to be okay.

When they pulled from the embrace, Sarah knelt down on one knee and addressed the dog, "Is this Masada?" she asked. She held out her palm for Masada to sniff. "Alex has told me wonderful things about you."

Masada proudly faced Sarah. She lifted her foot and rested her paw on Sarah's knee. The girl Alex remembered squealed in delight and took the paw that was offered.

"It's so nice to meet to you," she said and then looked up at Alex, "She's beautiful, Alex."

When Sarah stood up, Alex found his voice. "Let's get out of here." He snatched the only bag left, circling the conveyor belt. "We don't want to miss the graduation."

CHAPTER 34

The K9s For Warriors' first graduation brought out the entire town of Springfield. At least, to Alex it seemed that way. Various groups milled around in the exercise yard, where folding chairs had been planted in rows. The sun's warm rays melted the frost, but left the air crisp. A perfect day for new beginnings. A day no one would forget for a long time.

Alex and Sarah, with Masada at heel beside them, fell in line with Stacey, her daughter, and Daisy. Behind them trailed Steve and Rocky. They all forged ahead, weaving through the crowd. The people stepped aside, smiling cheerful greetings. "Good luck." "Congratulations." The teams plowed through to the front row of reserved seats and sat down, backs rigid, eyes forward.

Brad climbed the steps of a raised platform built for the occasion and sat down behind the podium. Next to him an American flag lifted in a slight breeze. Red, white and blue ribbons adorned the skirting around the stage while flags from each branch of service unfurled in the breeze. Judy, Carrie and Sue, the first puppy raisers of The K9s For Warriors, came on stage, and sat center stage behind Brad.

The crowd murmured in low voices as if they attended a wedding or a funeral. "It's seems like the open house happened just yesterday," one person said. And another, "Look how much the puppies have grown."

Brad stood and approached the dais. "Everyone take a seat." Bodies shuffled and in a few moments everyone found a seat. "Welcome everyone! What a glorious day this is! Judy Howard, a master trainer, certified by the Assistance Dog Association is responsible for the mature, well behaved dogs you see here today. Many of you met them as puppies. The transformation is stunning, don't you think?" The crowd responded with a loud, "Yes!"

Judy joined Brad. "Thank you all for coming," she said as she scanned the audience. "I could not have done this alone. Without Brad's vision and donation of the land, we would not be here today. Here is a man who had a dream and who had the courage and determination to make it become a reality." The crowd applauded. Judy raised her hands asking for quiet. "And without all of you, this program would not survive. There are so many other people to thank." She praised the main participants and donors of the program. All received powerful rounds of applause. "And let's not forget the men at the Taylorville Correctional

Facility who have also played a critical role in the training of these dogs." The crowd clapped again.

"Now, without further ado, the time has come to show you the miracles that have been created by your efforts. Let's meet the first teams to graduate from The K9s for Warriors." The deafening roars, hoorahs and applause pulsated in waves and faded across the fertile Illinois landscape.

Sweat crept down Alex's neck and sneaked between his shoulder blades. He wanted to kiss Mother Nature for the breeze that cooled the wet band of his hat. He stared straight ahead. He dared not meet Sarah eyes. The sight of her beside him, on this day, after all they'd been through….

He had made it. He was under the wire. He had survived. In Iraq, each time he returned from a mission, when he stepped back under the wire to safety, he had thanked whatever powers controlling the universe for the precious opportunity to make a difference, one more day. Today, he did the same.

"Ladies and gentlemen, I want you to meet our first team, Alex March, USMC and his service dog, Masada."

The crowd roared and Sarah squeezed his hand. He thought he'd lose it right then and there. He stood and whispered a command to Masada, unheard because of the crowd's enthusiasm. Man and dog marched up the stairs, onto the stage and took their place beside Judy.

On Judy's cue, Carrie rose, removed a vest from a box behind her chair, and approached Alex and Masada. Carrie addressed the warrior. "Alex, as the first graduate of the K9s for Warriors program, I want to personally congratulate you. Please, remove Masada's vest." Alex knelt down and his hands shook as he unbuckled the vest. He handed the used training uniform to Judy who turned back to the audience.

Holding it up to the crowd, Judy said, "Masada's vest says, Service Dog in training." She laid the vest a side. "This vest, and her new vest, was made from one of Alex's own uniforms. Each was sewn individually and donated by Sue's mother, Alice, the District Attorney's wife." Judy asked Alice to stand and take a bow and then motioned for Carrie to raise the new vest up high. "The gold embroidery on Masada's new vest says, 'Masada, Service Dog.' The crowd roared again.

Judy took the vest from Carrie and approached Masada, who stood, head held high. "Congratulations, Masada. You are now officially an American Service Dog. You are a professional. Throughout your training you have proved capable to stand ready and never quit. I am confident you will serve your comrade with loyalty and love. From this day forward you will never have to leave Alex's side."

The crowd exploded. Judy assisted Alex, whose hands trembled as he fumbled to buckle the vest.

Their moist eyes met a brief moment before they stood and shook hands. "Congratulations Alex. The K9's for Warriors wants to thank you for your service and for you and your family's sacrifices. We hope, with Masada's help, you can live your life to the fullest. " A rumble erupted from the crowd again, and as they applauded this time, they rose to their feet. Several deep "Oorah's" boomed over the din.

Masada's eyes riveted on Alex's. This time he was sure she smiled proudly at him. Then she turned her head back to the audience, and held her head even higher.

Judy waited for the audience to settle. Alex led Masada back to his seat, shaking Stacey's and Steve's hands as he moved past them and sat down. Sarah leaned over and kissed him on his cheek. His stomach curdled last night's dinner, yet he wanted to throw his cap into the air.

A wonderment swept over him. Masada was under his command now. He held her life in his hands. These hands. Pain stabbed his stomach. He thought of what his hands had done. He stared down at them now clutching Masada's leash. His heart would burst if it hammered any harder. Fear pulsated through his veins. *Deep breaths. Focus on the present. But tomorrow. What about tomorrow?* There had already been so many tomorrows. He focused on the ceremony. He was not going to lose control now.

Stacey did not hide her tears as she cried all the way back to her seat. She sat down next to Alex and he took her trembling hand. When she looked up at him, a tempest stormed in her siren eyes and he knew she, too, struggled with the responsibilities that lie ahead. They averted their gazes and stood as Steve and Rocky approached. Stacey hugged him. "Good luck Steve," she said, as she choked down more joyful sobs. Alex stood to shake his hand and grasp the warrior's shoulder. Pulling him close, they exchanged powerful hugs.

The sound of shuffling feet pulled their attention back to the stage and the new team members sat down. The children from the West Grand Elementary School choir were thumping onto the platform and taking their places. When the school's band struck the first cords of "God Bless America," the young voices burst into song. Already moved to tears by the effects of the ceremony, the emotional crowd stood and joined the children in song.

At the end of the performance, Judy rose clapping and approached the podium. She raised her voice above the crowd's enthusiasm. "There is one more team member I would like you to meet. Some of you might remember Boise, our fourth bumbling puppy from twenty months ago?" She motioned for Sue, who had been Boise's puppy raiser, to come up on the stage. Boise had grown into a fully developed male dog like Rocky. "Sometimes the puppies do not pass the strict requirements that are necessary to become a service dog. Boise was one of those dogs." The crowd settled. "Although Boise lacked the serious personality needed to become a service dog, we discovered he still loved to work and he loves children." Boise kept twisting his attention back toward the children in the choir.

"Boise has become a facility dog at the women's shelter. He lives at the shelter offering comfort and friendship to abused children. Some of the children come to the facility so traumatized by life situations that they refuse to talk." Judy motioned to Sue who removed Boise's lead.

"Boise why don't you go over and visit with Lucas? I know you are dying to say 'Hi' to your friend." Sue gave Boise a command and the dog bounded over to a small boy in the choir who squealed and broke away from the other children. The child wrapped his arms around Boise who gyrated with joy and leaped into the boy's embrace. The audience sat in awed silence as boy and dog became lost in their own world, oblivious to their surroundings.

"Ladies and gentlemen I'd like to introduce you to Lucas' grandmother, Molly Rivera."

A woman with grey streaked hair that disappeared into a tightly wrapped bun labored up the stairs. The crowd seemed to hold its breath, the only sound, the boy's chatter to the dog. The grandmother approached Judy, her arms out, and embraced her tightly. Murmuring softly, she said to Judy. "Thank you. Thank you so much." The two women finally pulled apart, each wiping their eyes and then the old woman faced the crowd.

"My Lucas, that you see there chattering away to the dog, came to the women's shelter after witnessing his mother, my daughter, beaten nearly to death by his father, who is now in prison for his crime. My daughter still suffers from her injuries, but she asked me to come here today. As a result of his trauma, my Lucas refused to talk and hated to be touched." Molly paused and glanced back at her grandson. The boy still chattered to the dog while Boise listened intently, the two, like long lost friends, reunited.

"After only three days with Boise on the premises, Lucas decided to reach out and trust again, even if it was only a dog." Molly took a deep breath to control her emotions. "Look at Lucas now. This dog they call Boise has performed a miracle. Lucas is now back in school and enjoying his boyhood again. I want everyone to be aware of what these dogs can do. If it weren't for the K9s For Warriors program I'm afraid to imagine what would have become of my grandson."

She turned to Judy and hugged her again. The crowd clapped timidly, perhaps afraid to startle the boy and dog. Obvious the boy and dog were

wrapped up in a reality of their own, the onlook-
ers rose up, their eyes blurred by their tears, and
clapped unendingly.

Judy raised her hand, a gesture for quiet, and
pointed. "Everyone, there's plenty of food inside
the training room, just go through those doors.
Get yourself something to eat and don't forget to
stop at the donations table. Everything you have
witnessed here is possible because of your generosity of time and money. In an hour we will meet
back here and introduce you to our next group of
puppies.

Stacey, Steve and Alex stuck together as audience members came up to congratulate and thank
them for their service. The admirers moved to the
puppy area to coo and awe over the next group of
future service dogs. When the pups had to take
their naps, the towns people, also tired from an
emotional day, returned to their cars, and volunteers began cleaning up to prepare for the next
new team of miracles.

CHAPTER 35

Alex's eyes sprang open. Once again, the dawn, unguarded, had slipped into his room and illuminated the drapery's gold embroidered edges. Careful not to wake Sarah, he rolled to his side and lifted his head slightly, to check on Masada. She lay, head on her paws, on the floor beside him. She, too, slept peacefully. He eased back facing Sarah and studied her as she slept. Her lids fluttered over the emerald green eyes that had searched his soul last night and allowed him entrance into hers.

He and Sarah had sat cross-legged on the bed and talked deep into the night. "I was wrong, Alex, about so many things," she had begun.

"No Sarah…"

She laid her fingers to his lips. "Hush, Alex. Let me say my piece. All this time, I worried about the part of you that hadn't come home, the part I wanted, that I missed. I was so angry and hurt and afraid I had lost you." She lowered her eyes, as if ashamed, and continued almost in a whisper.

"I realized a part of you had been left behind in Iraq. That was the boy I fell in love with. That boy laughed and played and yet, was afraid of nothing... well, except me, at first." She raised her eyes, peered through her lashes, and smiled. "That boy I knew was full of pride and good intentions...and so much love."

"Oh Sarah..." Alex reached to embrace her, but she leaned back and held his arms.

"Please Alex. Hear me out. That boy I knew was gone, and it frightened me. The more afraid I became, the more the anger consumed me. I was so selfish. I never asked why. I was afraid to know. I thought there might be someone else. I was locked up in my own prison with fears of what I had lost, of how I was going to make it without you, and I couldn't escape." Her fingers fiddled with her simple wedding band. Again, she looked up at him.

"Sarah, please. There's no one else." His thoughts flew to Stacey. "I can't say I didn't think about it. I did." He leaned in and held her face in his hands. Their eyes locked. "I am so glad I didn't. It's only you I want. It's always been just you...you and Aiden."

Alex released her and leaned back. He continued to stare as his brain shuffled around his wife's confessions, trying to make sense of them. She was afraid? She was angry? How had he not considered what she might be going through? He thought he knew what she wanted – A brave, proud Marine, afraid of nothing. Yet, here she was, still, though clearly he was none of those things.

"I was so wrong about you, Alex. True, you are not the boy I married, but, whether you realize it or not, you are still the proud, brave Marine I married. You are the bravest, strongest man I know." She wiped a tear that trickled down her cheek. "The other wives at the vet center made me understand what kind of battle you are still facing. I'm ashamed I haven't been there to support you."

It was Alex who hung his head now. "I should have admitted what I was going through," he said. "But how could I? I wouldn't even admit it to myself. For a long time I didn't even understand why I was acting like I did. I thought I was crazy. And I thought if I went for help it meant I was admitting I was crazy." He grabbed her hands. "I needed you so badly, and yet I was afraid you would see how weak I was, that you wouldn't respect me. I was so afraid of losing you."

"I'm here for you, Alex. Please, don't worry about me. Come home. We'll get through this together."

"I'm not ready to come home yet." He saw the surprise and then the disappointment shadow her eyes. "I can't come home until I'm certain I won't lose it and hurt you or Aiden. I've only had Masada two weeks and, yes, she has made such a difference, but I have to be sure." He held his breath waiting for her anger to flare.

Her expression remained determined. "I understand. I want you to be sure. I have faith in you, but you have to believe in yourself." She grabbed his hand and smiled. "Just don't forget, we're a team, too."

Alex exhaled and squeezed her hand. "I won't forget, I just have to be sure." They had kissed and held each other in the darkness. Their confessions freed them and the night became a sweet reunion.

And now, here she was. She slept soundly, unaware and trusting he will be there for her. She had been a school boy's dream and, now, she lived in his soul and her name would float out on his last breath when he grew old. Even buried beneath the soil he was certain his dried heart would flutter and rejoice at the sound of her footsteps.

Tomorrow they would fly home. Yes, he was frightened, but now he had a company of support behind him. So many had been involved. Miraculously they had brought him back from, not only the dark pit of suicide, but also from the fiery rage of murder. He would live to fight another day. He and Sarah had survived the first siege of the long invisible battle that faced them. A dog named Masada had led them home. He was back under the wire.

Oorah!

CHAPTER 36

Alex stood at the passenger loading – unloading area at the airport. The brisk October air cooled his neck as the perspiration leaked down his temples. He shook Judy's hand and said a simple goodbye to her, the one individual who had been responsible in pushing him to the top of the waiting list for his service dog. Immense humility and gratitude struck him mute and made his knees weak. In only two weeks Masada had made a tremendous difference in his life.

Judy reached up, hugged him and said, "Brad used his rank as Chief of Police and arranged for you, Masada, and Sarah to bypass airport security," Judy explained. "It's a luxury you won't have during your Dallas layover."

Alex nodded. Fear had been a constant companion since he arrived stateside. Funny how the emotion ruled him here on home soil. In Iraq, he lived in the moment with no time for the debilitating despair, only reaction to it. Today, he knew what frightened him. It was the future, leaving the safety of the K9s For Warriors and all those who had helped him and gave him so much hope, and starting his new life with his service dog.

Since Masada's first night with him two weeks ago, she continually woke him, interrupting the ugly angst of his nightmares. But his hope dipped and bobbled like a buoy in a storm. His dreams of becoming honorable and trustworthy once were still dim, but now they had begun to pulsate brighter.

Sarah bent down to the van's window and said her farewells to Judy while Masada leaned against Alex's leg. Finally, Sarah straightened and said, "We better go. Or we'll miss our flight."

Alex floated from the magic of last night's reunion, yet every time he thought of the significance of his wife's presence he choked up. Because of Masada, his marriage might be saved. To gain control, he pushed back the euphoria, tucked his duffle under his arm, and grasped the handle on her bag. "Okay. Let's go."

Inside, they took up their wait in the row of seats against a wall of windows. Alex crouched forward, elbows on his knees, and scratched Masada's ears while he monitored the flow of travelers moving about the gate area. No one's eyes but his own darted through the crowds. No one stood out. His knee bopped up and down. The middle easterners he scrutinized didn't appear suspicious. They were probably students, political interns or aides.

Still, he wondered about the degree of security in such a small airport.

Beside him, Sarah studied the literature in Masada's tote bag. She wore the silk sweats with the hot pink stripe down the leg. Alex's hormones stirred as he recalled the outfit crumpled on their bedroom floor after she had forgiven him for one of his PTSD episodes. A lifetime ago. He flushed, surprised he had allowed his mind to wander.

"You have to send in monthly report forms," she said.

"Yes, I know." Alex continued to monitor the airport's activity. A man yelled at someone running. He stiffened. Masada raised her head. His mind flashed back to a hot day in Iraq. He stood sentry as he waited for a copter to airlift the injured from a firefight. His pulse quickened to the thump-thump of the copter's blades and the shouts of his team leader. Masada nudged his arm. He glanced down, reminded that this was the Springfield Airport.

"Oh, did you see her puppy album!" Sarah shoved the photos onto Alex's lap. He gritted his teeth at the distraction and petted Masada, who sat between his knees. Her sable eyes met his, his heartbeat slowed and the invisible situation neutralized. He drew his attention back to the album on his lap.

"She was a cute puppy, wasn't she?" he said, as he put his arm around Sarah. "I wish I had watched her grow up." He pointed to the sudsy picture of himself, giving Masada a bath, and laughed. "We'll set up regular appointments at the grooming salon as soon as we get home."

In Dallas, Alex sought an exit leading outside for Masada to perform her duties. Re-entering required them to again pass through security. Alex began to follow Sarah through the detector when a freckled faced guard stepped between them "You have to wait, sir." The boy motioned for another official.

What the...? All these security jerks were either punks or so old and fat they couldn't stop a grandma with a club. Alex had already seen them pass two, twenty five year old middle easterners through without any interrogation. Sarah, already cleared, collected her belongings from the plastic bin on the conveyor. Realizing Alex wasn't behind her, she looked up. She started toward him. Alex raised his hand and shook his head with a flash of irritation. Her lips tightened and she stopped and turned away. She was always trying to come to his rescue. Masada sat patiently by his side.

The second official arrived, fifty pounds overweight and couldn't see his own belt buckle. He approached with his superior in tow, whose stick-boy build swam in his wrinkled uniform. The trio faced Alex. Stick-boy spoke. "May I see your ID?"

Alex's blood pounded in his temples as he fished out his passport and handed it to the thin man.

What's your destination, sir?" Beer belly grasped his belt and yanked up on his pants.

"Ontario, Ca. sir."

"Has anyone asked you to hold or watch their bag for them?" Stick boy studied the passport.

Alex shifted his weight and clamped his jaw. The familiar touch of Masada's nose nudged against his hand. He released his fist. "No, sir."

"Did you pack your own bag?" Beer belly was probably wondering if it was lunch time.

"Yes sir."

Stick boy peered down at Masada and her sable eyes met his. He paused, his face softened, as if charmed by her attentive stare. He didn't ask for her certification. Instead he drew up to his full height, returned his focus to Alex, and handed back the passport. "Your papers seem in order. Have a nice day."

"Thank you, sir." Alex sighed deeply, his anger drained away. The trio dispersed and Alex reached down. Petting Masada, he said, "Let's go."

The drone of the jet's engines made the last leg of the journey drag. Sarah dozed, warm against him, Masada lay at his feet, but Alex could not surrender to sleep. He considered the new phase of his life about to begin. Soon he would be able to live a normal life with Sarah and Aiden. Normal.

What was normal? Masada had only been with him for two weeks. How could he trust himself not to fly into a rage over another angry driver incident or a semi's air horn? He had shared with Kevin that he didn't feel comfortable moving back with Sarah until he was sure. "I get it buddy," Kevin said. "It was a while before I trusted that Diego would always be there for me. It was too good to be true."

The orientation had only lasted two weeks, but it seemed a lifetime. He had not thought of another tour since the day his counselor, Mark Parrish, had given him the news about receiving a service dog. And how long had he been without a drink? He recalled Sarah's surprise when he had not hit the bar at the terminal. Had the dog done all this? Sarah's sleeping form stirred him with more than hope.

Her face, soft in sleep, reassured him. But it was Masada's presence, her head resting solidly on his boot, that overwhelmed him. The dog's genuine love offered what humans could never master, unconditional love. During these two weeks he had learned that if the dog was calm, it calmed him. Her devotion, her intensive training, made her existence in his life huge. Tears blurred his vision each time, as they did now, when he thought of what Masada meant to him.

They landed in California at the Ontario airport and disembarked without incident, then proceeded outside to the pickup area. Alex caught sight of Kevin waving from the drop-off and pick-up area.

When they met, Kevin shook Alex's hand, pounded his shoulder. Grabbing Sarah's bag, Kevin tossed it in the trunk, and said, "Welcome home, buddy." Leaving the trunk open, he opened the passenger door for Sarah. "Sarah and I rescued your truck from a huge bill in long term parking. It's at my place. This is my folks Camry." He jumped back in the driver's seat.

Alex nodded, threw his duffle in the trunk, and slammed it shut. He ordered Masada to squeeze into the backseat with Diego and he followed her in. Kevin swiveled around to the back seat and eyed Masada. "Well, hello girl. It's nice to meet you." He gave her a quick pat on the head. "Diego will be glad to have a playmate." The dogs touched noses in greeting. Diego sat obediently on the seat, Masada on the floorboard. Kevin turned back, gunned the accelerator and said, "Let's get out of this madhouse."

Kevin eyes met Alex's in the rear view mirror as he pulled from the curb. "How was the flight? "

Alex figured his buddy was trying to ease the tension with small talk, keep the conversation light. So much had gone unsaid since Alex had left for Illinois. "It was smooth," he said. "Sarah slept all the way. Wish you had been there, to have someone to talk to." He reached over and flipped Kevin's cap.

"Hey! I'm driving here. You better not cause a crash. Just cause you're friends with the Chief of Police in Springfield isn't going to get you out of anything here in California."

When they pulled up to Sarah's parents' house, Aiden came running out the front door. "Daadee!" The boy jumped into his father's arms. As the Fredricks approached, Alex hugged the boy, reluctant to let go and strap him to his car seat. Sarah's mom peered through the window into the back seat. "I can't wait to meet your new dog. She looks like Diego. I know you guys are tired from the trip. You'll have to come by tomorrow."

From the passenger seat Sarah said, "Yes, mom, it's been a long day. Thanks for watching him." Sarah threw her folks a kiss. "I'll call you tomorrow."

Reaching out, Alex shook Mr. Frederick's hand. "Thank you sir, for everything. You know, Sarah's plane ticket and, well just everything."

Mr. Fredericks nodded and turned to his wife, "Come on, mom. These young folks need to get home." He put his arm around his wife's waist and herded her back to the house.

Alex paused for a moment watching Sarah's parents walk away. They had survived their untold stories, he only hoped he and Sarah could do the same.

The old couple waved from the front porch as Kevin pulled away. Throughout the drive across town, Alex's heart swelled, listening to his son babble to the two dogs. This is why he hadn't pulled the trigger that desperate night, a lifetime ago.

Sarah smiled. Relief smoothed her features. Maybe everything was going to be okay. "What are we doing for dinner?" she asked. They agreed a barbeque in the back yard would be a great way for the dogs and Aiden to get acquainted.

At Sarah's, in the backyard, Kevin cooked the burgers, keeping an eye on Aiden and the dogs, while Alex and Sarah sliced tomatoes, and prepared a salad inside.

Bringing out the condiments, Alex set them on the patio table as Kevin raised his beer in the air and pointed to a red cooler. "I was thinking of you, jarhead."

Alex lifted the lid. A twelve pack chilled in a bed of ice. "None for me. I quit." Alex's own words startled him. It was the first time he had said it out loud.

"What? You quit?" Kevin threw back the last swallow of the cold, gold liquid and licked his lips. "Really?" He stared at Alex.

Alex nodded. "It's been two weeks." The ice dripped off Kevin's beer. Hs mouth watered.

Sarah brought out the plates and napkins. Her back stiffened when she noticed the cooler.

Kevin shook his head. "Sorry, Bud, I didn't know." He tossed his empty bottle into the recycle bin.

"It's okay." Alex's shoulders slumped. He was going to miss the good times at the Ponderosa and the Paint Ball Park.

Kevin shook his head and turned back to the grill. "Burgers are done."

Autumn air chilled the afternoon. Diego chased his ball, and Masada her bunny, while Aiden laughed and screamed, chasing after the dogs. After dinner when Aiden turned fussy, Alex got him ready for bed, then helped Sarah clean up the kitchen. When he could put it off no longer, he hugged her goodbye. "I'll check in with you tomorrow after my counseling appointment."

"I wish you were staying."

Sarah trusted him. He was the only one who didn't.

CHAPTER 37

Kevin maneuvered the car out of Sarah's driveway into light traffic. Alex sat shotgun, his arm rested on the open window. With an intense look, Kevin glanced at Alex. "Look, Alex. About what I said about Sarah and me…"

"Let it go, Kevin." Alex stared straight ahead. "I always knew. I just didn't want to face it." Alex lifted his cap and ran his fingers through his short cropped hair. "And it was always okay, because I knew you wouldn't cross that line. I trusted you."

Alex looked at Kevin, who kept his eyes on the road. "Look, I know I was going crazy, I couldn't stop. I was being such a shithead. I wouldn't have blamed either of you. It's me who should apologize." Alex turned back and focused on the passing scenery. "If something ever happens to me I want you to be there for her."

Kevin accelerated onto the freeway. He squirmed, obviously uncomfortable with the strong sentiments. "Hey nothin's going to happen to either one of us." He reached over and punched Alex's shoulder. "We'll both be old men in our rockers on the porch while your grandkids are yelling and the dogs are barking. You'll be reading one of my many, New York Times bestselling, crime novels that I gleaned from your career as a detective."

"I just want you to know, in case something ever happens." The ride continued, Alex lost in his thoughts. Kevin's silence proved, he too, mulled over the future.

When Kevin turned into his folk's ranch, Alex felt a familiar pull, aware he missed the place, especially the mare, Miss Belle, and Spider Cat. The horses studied the car as it crept down the long drive. In front of the bunkhouse, Spider Cat raised his head from his usual curled position in the rocking chair. Two weeks had been a lifetime.

Alex climbed out, followed by Masada as he yanked his duffle from the trunk. "See you tomorrow, buddy." He started toward the bunkhouse when Kevin called out. "Good to have you back, Bud, and congratulations, Masada's a great dog."

Alex nodded. "See you at the center."

Spider Cat slipped between his legs and dashed inside the cabin, escaping the slamming screen door just as he had done what seemed like so long ago. Already comfortable with Diego, the cat touched his nose to Masada's, who had received her cat training from Judy's cat, Sportster.

Alex dropped his duffle on the floor and stretched out on the bed. With his arms behind his head, he studied the shadows moving across the ceiling as the sun set. He was almost home. Spider Cat climbed up and began kneading his chest with soft paws. He recalled that desperate, suicidal night and realized it was Spider Cat who had distracted him from pulling the trigger. And Miss Belle. The mare had needed him when it felt like no one else did. All that was a lifetime ago. Finally he rose, "Come on Masada, lets meet Miss Belle and we'll go for a run."

Alex strode through the doors of the vet center with Masada by his side. He was scheduled for a brief meeting with Mark Parrish before the group began.

"So this is your new team member?" Mark said as he came out of his office. He knelt down in front of the dog. "What's his name?"

"It's Masada. And he's a she." Alex squatted down. "Greet, Masada." She offered her paw to Mark.

Mark took the dog's foot. ""It's great to meet you, girl. I know you two will make a great team." He stood. "Come on in, Alex. Have a seat." Mark took his place behind his desk. "I've been looking over your file. You missed two weeks of classes. Do your professors think you will be able to catch up?"

"I think so, sir. I'm sure going to try."

"I don't want to throw a wrench in your plans, Alex, but now that you have a service dog, things will be different."

Alex's stomach twisted. "What do you mean? It's already different … better. I mean, it's only been two weeks, but the migraines and the nightmares have lessened. The flash backs still happen, but I don't seem to go as deep, and I come back faster. I haven't moved back home yet, I want to be sure."

"That's wise, but I'm talking about your career choice. I know how committed you are to becoming a police officer, but with a service dog and being diagnosed with PTSD, well, it might not be a realistic goal."

The blood in Alex's temples pulsed. *What the…?* Now that everything is coming together they're going to use it against me? "I don't understand, sir. I been going to counseling. I really feel I'm getting a handle on the PTSD."

"I've checked into the regulations for the police academy. You are required to do at least a year on patrol before you could be promoted to detective. Even if you could handle the pressure and stress, which I think is a good possibility, because you've made good progress, but I don't know of any cop who patrols with a service dog."

The ringing in Alex's ears muted the counselor's words so only his lips moved. Alex had chosen police work because he liked the challenge. He hadn't considered anything else. Solving crimes. Justice. Making a difference.

Mark was still talking. "Look, give it some thought. Right now you don't even trust yourself to go home to your family. Do you know what you would do if you got a call that ended in a gun-fight? All I'm saying is finish your classes. Don't panic. You've got time to figure it out. We'll talk about it more next week."

Alex stood and forced himself to shake the psychologist's hand. "Thank you, sir." *Yeah, thanks for nothing.*

During the group session, Alex passed when it was his turn to share. At the break, Alex felt Kevin's puzzled stare, but his friend didn't press him. When the group broke up, Alex rushed to his truck as Masada trotted alongside to keep up.

He drove without a destination. His fist pounded the steering wheel. When he saw Masada's claws dig into the seat as he took a turn too fast, he braked. Guilt brought back some sort of reason and he slowed down. He was surprised when he found himself in the Ponderosa's parking lot. He stared at the door. The same bikers from a lifetime ago sat on their bikes chugging beers and smoking. He rolled down the window and lit a cigarette. Why is it, since he came home from Iraq, nothing's been easy? Nothing. I thought it would be easier with the dog. He looked over at

Masada. She turned toward him as if asking, "What are you going to do, Marine?"

Fuck it. He pushed open the truck door. "Let's go." Masada trotted to keep up. He inhaled the last deep drags from his smoke as he strode toward the entrance, pinched it off, and tossed it. He slammed his body against the door and pushed into the darkness.

He grabbed a stool at the end of the bar and ordered Masada to lay down. The bartender evaluated his customer with a hard stare, "What'll it be?

CHAPTER 38

Alex stared at the bartender as he mentally added up his days of sobriety. Eighteen. Eighteen lousy days. Eighteen miraculous days.

"What's it gonna be? The usual?" The bartender said, stone-faced since the night Alex took out that farmer with a choke hold.

Screw them all. "Yeah, the usual." It didn't matter what the usual was. He ached for the alcoholic relief from constant disappointment. The bartender grabbed a cold one, popped the top, and slid the bottle in front of him. The beer dripped with melting ice and puddled on the bar. The Ponderosa was the only bar he knew that kept cold beer on ice. Alex curled his fingers around it.

"This is the last place I thought I'd find you." He jumped as Kevin appeared behind him and sat his bulk down on the stool next to him. "Why'd you rush out? I needed to talk to you."

Alex firmed up his grip on the drink as if Kevin might seize it. He might have known Kevin would show up here, it was his favorite watering hole, too. He hadn't quit drinking. "What's it to you?"

He swallowed hard. His throat was dry, his stomach roiled, and his brain begged for the elixir. "What do you want to talk about? If it's about me being here, mind your own business."

"Boy aren't you miss bitchy?" Kevin laughed as he took a long swallow from the beer the bartender set in front of him. "Do what you want, Marine. I'm not your mother." He wiped his mouth with his sleeve and exhaled, as if taunting him. "It about Dave. Remember, him? I just got a text from his dad. He's in the county jail on suicide watch. His dad says we were Dave's only friends. Could we go talk to him?"

"I thought he was on tour."

"His hummer got hit and his entire team was taken out except him. They diagnosed him with TBI and sent him home. He hadn't been home long when his wife kicked him out because he got abusive, and now, she's suing for child support. While he was waiting for the VA to straighten out his benefits and medical, the court garnished his paycheck, so then, he couldn't pay his rent."

"So, what's he in for?" Alex slid his fingers up and down the cold bottle.

"Spousal abuse, non-payment of child support, and threatening a police officer. His dad says Dave's begging him to bail him out but he's afraid to. He's worried what he might do." Kevin's focus riveted on Alex. "You need to go talk to him."

Alex stared at the beer in front of him as if the brew held answers to his life, Dave's life, and the world's problems. He turned to Kevin. "Why me?" He wanted to be left alone.

"He's a Marine. We take care of our own."

"You're a Marine, too. You help him."

Kevin stood up and faced Alex. "Look Jarhead. Whatever bug is up your ass, get over it. You know what he's going through. You can help. You have to reach out to a fellow comrade. Come on, let's move out."

Alex shook his head. "What the hell." He shoved the beer away and threw a fiver on the bar. "Let's go."

He remembered the clang of the bars, the shuffle of the shackles. This time he was visiting one of his own. Alex sat in front of the thick window and picked up the phone. Masada lay calmly at his feet. On the other side, Dave shuffled through a door followed by other inmates. Unlike the others, Dave wore a stiff canvas smock and was barefoot. The door sealed shut with a thunk and solid clank. The image of Roy and the other veteran inmates Alex had met in Illinois came to mind. He wondered how many were vets here. He didn't know why he had come here. He didn't know what he could say. Dave sat down and faced him on the other side of the glass. Alex put the phone to his ear and tried to feign levity. "Hey, Marine, how's brig life?"

Dave picked up his receiver. "There's no privileges like we had at the FOB, but it smells the same." His smile was forced. "At least there's no airstrikes. I can handle these homies in here and their shivs. They're amateurs."

"What can I do for you? You need anything?" Alex wondered if they had a dog training program.

Dave leaned up to the glass and tried to peer down past Alex. "What's that? You finally got a service dog? Good for you. Kevin told me you're doing good."

Alex flushed in embarrassment. His career problems suddenly seemed small. "Yeah, I guess. I got lucky … getting the dog. You know I came so close to being where you are? I'm sorry for you, man. What can I do? You got a lawyer?"

"I don't need one. I don't really care anymore. My future isn't too bright. I'm facing five to ten if the charges stick. Anyway, it's over between Rhonda and me. She'll never let me see the kids again, and I don't blame her. They're afraid of me. And the Corps will never clear me to go back. I wish I'd gone out with my team. At least they all died heroes."

Alex hung his head. "Man you can't talk like that."

"Didn't you hear what I said?" Dave yelled and the guards tensed. "My kids are fucking afraid of me!" Dave's face reddened and his white knuckles gripped the receiver.

Alex looked around as if someone might be listening. "I almost pulled the trigger myself. You got to hang on. Who's your attorney? I'll see what I can do to help."

Dave hung his head. "It's Eric Bassinger. He's a public defender. He's gathering my information to submit it to the Veteran's Treatment Court." He laughed, but his face sneered, contorting his youthful appearance. "I told him treatment is not going to help my sorry ass. All they wanted to do at the VA is feed me a bunch of pills. I told him to take his do-gooder's ass and go save someone else."

"What about Rhonda? And the kids? You want me to check on them?" Alex tried to come up with a way to help this fallen Marine get back under the wire.

"You've got to be kidding me? She's why I'm here." Dave laughed even louder, yet his eyes welled with tears. "I told you it's over. That's never going to happen."

"I was sure of the same thing with Sarah, less than a month ago. Miracles happen, you gotta keep the faith." He automatically glanced down at Masada.

Dave's face twisted grotesquely. "Look. Don't feed me any girly bullshit. I'm no God dammed recruit. I know where I stand." He pounded his fist on the counter, but jerked around when he heard the clicking of the guards' shotguns. He spun back, steeled against his anger, and shoved his fists in his lap. He lowered his voice to a whisper. "I've seen others give up the fight. If I get a chance, I'll do the same. I'll end everyone's misery, Dad's, Rhonda's, my kids who are afraid of me, and mine."

Alex face burned and his lips straight-lined. He glared at Dave. He heard his teeth grinding. An uncontrollable rage erupted and he jumped from his chair, thankful for the barrier between them. Masada scrambled to her feet. "You are not going AWOL, Marine! No surrender! Marines don't quit." He was the one yelling now. He threw the phone against the glass, swung around and searched for the exit.

CHAPTER 39

He slammed his body against the heavy metal door. It opened slowly into the visitor's waiting room. He stormed past Kevin, jerked his arm, and motioned for him to follow. "Let's get out of here."

Out in the daylight, Masada, Kevin and Diego trotted to keep up with their agitated comrade. "How'd it go? How's he doing?"

A myriad of emotions churned in Alex's head. He tried to shove the bile down. Dizzy with fear for Dave, his steps faltered. He understood exactly where the guy was, and if he didn't figure out what to do, his friend would succeed in taking himself out. Helplessness turned his legs to jelly. He reached the truck exhausted and out of breath, and leaned against the fender.

"He's not." He pulled out a cigarette, lit it, and drew in a deep drag.

"He's not what?" Kevin studied his friend.

"He's not doing well!" Kevin flinched as Alex exhaled and immediately sucked in another long line of smoke. "He's determined to cash it in. I don't know what to do."

Kevin met his buddy's stare. "Did you tell him you've been in his boots? That he can't give up? That Marines don't surrender, ever?"

Alex swung around and yanked open the driver's door. "Yeah, of course I did! Let's get out of here." Masada, Kevin and Diego scrambled in.

Alex burned rubber out of the parking lot and turned left.

Kevin grabbed the dash. "Hey take it down a notch, will ya? Where're we going?"

"We're going to pay Rhonda a visit."

"Do you think that's wise? She's the one trying to take him down."

"If she doesn't come around, he's a dead man walking."

"I guess it can't hurt. All she can do is throw us out."

"She's going to listen."

"I take it back. All she can do is call the cops on us."

The little house reminded Alex of his and Sarah's. A bike with training wheels rested against a leafless elm in the front yard. The brown grass had given up growing at ankle height. The peeling paint predicted abandonment.

Alex parked. He glared at the house. A car sat in the drive. Through the car's rear window two car seats peeked up. "She's home. Come on."

Alex banged on the door. Movement scuffled inside.

A small child called out. "Mom! Someone's here."

A chain rattled, a deadbolt clicked, and the door cracked open. Alex motioned to Kevin to step back away from the door. "Rhonda?"

"Yes?"

I'm Alex, and this is Kevin. I don't know if you remember us but we're friends of Dave. We'd like to talk to you."

"I remember. You gave Dave a lift to the Paint Ball Park several times. What did you want to see me about?"

"Could we come in? I promise we won't take up much of your time." Rhonda focused on Masada and Diego. "And the dogs, too, may they come in? They are trained service dogs. I assure you, they won't be a problem." A boy about Aiden's age squealed, squeezed through the crack and reached for Masada.

"Ricky. Be careful, the dogs might bite." Rhonda swung open the door and swept up her charge.

"Really, ma'am. The dogs are okay. They are trained to be calm and friendly in any circumstance." Kevin said.

Rhonda hiked Ricky onto her hip and nodded without enthusiasm. "Well, come on in."

The small living room was clean, but cluttered with toys. The men stepped around them as if they were IEDs and took a seat on the couch. Diego and Masada lay down at their feet unbothered by Ricky's older sister, Kimberly, who plopped down on her knees and began petting them. Rhonda stood staring, as Ricky fussed, twisting to be let down to join his sibling. "Okay, okay," she said, and let the toddler slide to the ground. Like a wind-up toy, he scooted across the hardwood floor toward the dog.

"What are their names, sir?" The little girl asked.

"This is Diego," Kevin said. "Diego, greet." Diego held up his paw to the small child, who giggled in response. "Hello, Deego." She grabbed his paw with her small pink hand.

Alex followed Kevin's lead. "And this is Masada." Masada too, greeted the little girl, ignoring Ricky who had begun to crawl on top of her.

"Hello, 'sada.' She is so soft." Kimberly wrapped her arms around the dog's neck and hugged her.

"I can't believe these kids," Rhonda said. "When strangers come in they are always hiding in the other room. And they're afraid of dogs."

"It's the dogs ma'am. They're specially trained. I think kids sense that. These dogs are kid magnets."

Rhonda shrugged, relaxed, as if glad her children were safe and occupied for the moment. She sank into a chair. "So what did you want to talk to me about?"

Alex and Kevin exchanged nervous looks. Alex took a deep breath and said, "It's about your husband, ma'am. It's about Dave. We were wondering if, well, maybe you could back off the charges. Give him some slack."

Rhonda stiffened, her soft, full lips disappeared into a thin, hard line. She stood up. "Kid's go to your room. You can watch Barney." With pouty faces they glanced first at the dogs, then at their mother. Kimberly's three-year old face became grown-up. "Come on Ricky." She took her little brother's hand. "The grown-ups have to talk." Rhonda herded them into their bedroom. Barney's singing muffled when she stepped out of the room, closed the door and returned to her chair.

Rhonda didn't sit down. She locked eyes with Alex. "I can't do that. I don't know what kind of spell you have on my kids, but since Dave's come home they've been withdrawn and won't talk to anyone, especially strangers. He'd been home less than a week when he almost killed my dad. He went crazy. He thought he was back in Afghanistan. I was screaming at him. The kids were huddled in a corner, watching. Thank God he came out of it. He apologized and begged me to forgive him, and I did.

"Not even a week later, we were at the mall and he attacked a guy who cut him off in the parking lot. Someone called the cops. It took five cops to take him down. It's a miracle they didn't shoot him. I bailed him out of jail with money from our savings.

"He accused me of cheating on him. Sometimes he wouldn't let me leave the house." She sank into the chair. "I couldn't take it anymore. He wasn't working. He hardly slept. He woke up from nightmares yelling, scaring the kids and me. I asked him to move out and he went crazy. I was able to rush into the bathroom lock the door and call the police. I had him arrested."

Alex hung his head. How could he blame her? "Have you or Dave gone to the VA for help? "

"Dave said he went, but I'm not sure if he really did."

"How about you, Rhonda? Did you seek help?"

She sprang up from her seat, her eyes grew large and tears swelled. "Me? Why should I go? I'm not the one going psycho. I got enough to do just trying to make ends meet and taking care of the kids."

Masada started to get up and approach Rhonda. Alex reminded her to lay down. "I'm sorry ma'am. I didn't mean to upset you." Alex knotted Masada's leash in his hand. He frowned and set his jaw." It's just that your husband is on suicide watch. You have to do something."

Her arms hugged her body. She wiped at her nose. "I gave him every chance I could. You're not going to put me on your self-sacrificing, Marine

Corps guilt trip. I've got my kids to think about. I think you should leave."

Masada stood and pulled again at her leash, trying to reach Rhonda. Alex released his grip and the dog approached her. Masada leaned against Rhonda and nuzzled her elbow. The coldness of her nose distracted the distraught woman and her eyes dropped down to Masada's. Rhonda held her gaze as did Masada, and then Rhonda's shoulders sagged, draining of tension. She raised her head and focused on the men before her. A deep tiredness shadowed her eyes as she slumped back into her chair. "What do you want me to do?"

CHAPTER 40

Alex pulled away from the curb.

Kevin checked his email on his phone. "Do you think she'll do it?"

"I don't know. I assured her he was receiving counseling, whether he liked it or not. The treatment court would make sure of that." Alex gunned the accelerator as he merged into freeway traffic. "If Rhonda visits him, maybe he won't give up hope."

Kevin studied his cell, then shoved it in his pocket. "Do you think she'll even talk to Sarah?" He glanced up. "Hey, you passed our exit. Where're you going now?"

"I'm going to visit Dave's public defender. I want to find out what I can do to help his case."

"How long is this going to take? I just got a text from one of Diego's fans from my journalism class. She says her shitzu wants to meet Diego at the dog park at four. I'm telling you this dog is a chick magnet." He reached back and patted Diego on the head. "For someone who didn't want to get involved, you are sure sinking your teeth into this.

So, what was your problem this morning? What got your panties in a wad?"

"Mark told me the police academy won't take veterans with service dogs. I guess I hadn't thought it through. If I'm sent out on a shootout, what's Masada going to do? Lick the perps? I don't even know what I'd do. At this point, I don't trust myself with my wife and kid. " Alex shot a glance at Kevin as he turned into the court parking lot. "I'll try not to keep Diego from his date."

"I understand, buddy. I was edgy after I first got Diego. I wanted to believe he would save my ass during a flashback or a nightmare. And he did during the two week training, but, still, once I took him home with me it was hard to trust he would come through every time." Kevin turned to Diego again. The dog rested alongside Masada. Both lay with their chins on their paws, eyes closed. "I trust him now. He's given me so much confidence. Sometimes, when I run to the store, I don't even take him. I never could have done that in the beginning."

"I can't imagine going anywhere without Masada. I realize I've got to look at other careers, but I like the criminal and justice systems."

"Does this mean no ride-a-longs to research my great American novel?"

Alex forced a smile. "I'll see if I can come up with something that's equally hair raising." Parking, he killed the engine. "Come on, let's find out what this Veteran Treatment Court is all about."

After going through the court house metal detectors and enduring the questions about Masada and Diego, Alex's head throbbed. Once he cleared security, he started to relax, but he felt like a rat in a maize as they sent them from one information booth to the next. Kevin kept checking his text messages as they wandered the court house halls. The historical building spread its wings across an entire city block.

A guard standing outside a closed courtroom recognized their frustration. "What are you folks trying to find?"

Kevin, desperate to get done and get to his dog park date, answered. "We're looking for Eric Petersen. He's a public defender."

The guard directed them to go back to the east wing and take the elevator to the third floor. "The PD's offices occupy most of that floor."

Alex whipped around and followed Kevin back the way they had come. "City government, U.S. government, no one knows anything." He slapped Masada's leash against his leg.

"At least there's no more metal detectors to pass through."

Alex pushed open the door with the frosted window and gold lettering, Eric Bassinger, Public Defender. He scanned the small, waiting area and stepped into the room. Straight back chairs lined one wall, leaving little room for the two men and their dogs. Alex approached the receptionist's window. He spoke into the hole in the Plexiglas, separating him from a receptionist, engrossed in stamping a pile of papers. "My name's Alex March, ma'am. I'm here to see Eric Bassinger, and this is Kevin Kirkpatrick."

The girl raised her head and blinked past bright orange bangs as she pushed her heavy black rimmed glasses up onto her narrow nose. "Do you have an appointment?" Noticing the dogs, she peered down at Masada and Diego, sitting beside the Marines. "What beautiful dogs." Her glasses slid back down her nose where they remained as she fingered a lock of hair and checked her clipboard. "You're not on the list."

"I'm sorry, ma'am. No, we don't. We're hoping to talk to him about one of his cases."

She focused on a man rushing into the reception area, carrying a briefcase and a volume of folders clamped under his arm. She smiled. "You're in luck. Here he comes now."

Eric Bassinger disappeared through a side door and reappeared behind the secretary. His loose blue tie sagged around his collar and his long sleeves were rolled up to his elbows. She swiveled her chair around to her boss, and said, "These men would like a few minutes with you. You have twenty minutes before you need to be back in court." She turned back to Alex. "Which case are you here about?"

"Dave Vargas, ma'am."

She raised her brow and twisted back to Eric. "He's the one on suicide watch."

Eric nodded, without looking up. "Show them in." He about faced and disappeared into the bowels of his office.

Eric stood behind his desk and stacked the folders on the desk's corner by shoving another pile toward its center. He still didn't look up. "Have a seat gentlemen. You've got twenty minutes." He pulled his cell phone from his jacket pocket, checked it, and set the device on an opened folder in front of him. "Sorry. Seventeen. What can I do for you?" He proceeded to unroll his sleeves and button the cuffs.

Alex and Kevin squeezed into the small space and sat on the two fold-up chairs, their knees pressed against the desk. "We want to know what we can do to help with the Dave Vargas's case."

Bassinger stopped shuffling his paperwork and looked up. "You want to help? In what way?" He sat down and considered the men before him, his eyes scanned the dogs.

"Well, first of all, we just came from talking to Mr. Vargas's wife, Rhonda. She's willing to visit him and make a statement on his behalf. We would like you to talk to her."

"Tell her to make an appointment."

"She's quite vulnerable, sir. And she has two kids. She would have to get a sitter. With all due respect, sir, I think you should jump on this. Before she changes her mind."

The public defender stared at Alex, then waved his hand over his desk. "Do you see these folders? Each one represents a case. Twenty involve veterans. For the veterans I am supposed to gather their information – medical records, statements from their family, their bosses, and commanding officers and submit it all to the Veterans Court Judge. The judge then decides if they qualify to stand before him, which means he can then rule to suspend their sentence until they receive treatment for their PTSD or TBI. He can also reinstate their parole, if it had been revoked, or he can decide if they need a substance abuse program. Most do."

Alex started to respond. "Yes sir, but…"

"Then, two months later, I have to follow up on all of them to insure each has fulfilled the judge's requirements. If they have, I can move the charges be suspended or dismissed, depending on the offense." He shook his head and leaned back in his chair.

"Most of the time these vets won't even talk to me. They don't think I understand their situation." He began pulling out folders from various stacks on his desk. "If you want to help, become a mentor."

"You won't go see her?" Irritated by the man's attitude, Alex began to stand. Masada, picking up on his agitation, stood, too. Kevin laid his hand on Alex's arm.

"I said, if you want to help, become a mentor." The public defender's words were clipped as he met Alex's stare.

"What's a mentor?" Kevin asked.

"Because of the veterans' trust issues, the treatment court has begun enlisting mentors to stand with the veteran before the judge. Mentors are volunteers, veterans themselves. It's a new program and there are not enough of them. As a mentor you can take her statement." He caught his breath and scrutinized Alex and Kevin. An awkward silence filled the tiny office.

"So, I'll repeat myself. Why don't you guys become his mentors? I have to be back in court. See Shari. She'll get you the names of who to contact." He stood up, snatched up his cell, and another volume of files. "I'm sorry gentlemen, I've got to go." He came around his desk and paused. "Service dogs, right?"

"Yes sir." The two men chimed and scrambled to stand up in the cramped quarters.

Eric knelt down and petted first Diego, then Masada. "I hear they're doing great work. I wish every vet could have one." He rose, shifted his load of folders and reached out and shook the men's hands. "It's been a pleasure," and dashed out the door.

CHAPTER 41

In the court's parking lot the men herded their dogs into the truck and climbed in. Alex glanced at Kevin. "I told Sarah I'd drop by. She expected me this morning and it's already noon. Do you want me to drop you off first?"

"That's okay. The dog park girl canceled. She's going to the mall with her girlfriends. Not my thing. Anyway, I gotta study. Got an essay to turn in tomorrow."

"Yeah, me too. I've got a lot of cramming to do to catch up. At least all my classes are basic. Whatever I decide to major in, I'm not wasting my time."

"Improvise, adapt, and overcome. That's what my buddy Clint would say." Kevin sat with his back to the passenger door and his arm over the seat, scratching Diego's ears.

"Eastwood got it from the Green Berets. Sarah's dad was Army Special Forces. He's always saying that.""

"No shit?" Kevin held up his fist "Thanks, bro. I better have my facts right for that great American novel I'm writing." Alex offered a tight grin and pounded Kevin's knuckles with his own. "He never told me he was a Green Beret."

"He didn't tell me either. Sarah told me." He pulled into the drive. "She says he never talks about it."

Sarah's screen door rattled as Alex rapped a couple times before pulling it open. "Sarah? " From the den, her melodic voice joined in with Aiden's. "Itsy Bitsy Spider…."

The singing stopped. "Dadeee!" The boy barreled into the kitchen and scrambled around the table.

Alex laughed at his son's enthusiasm and reached down to swing him up on his shoulders. "Hey, you Devil Pup. Daddy missed you." But the boy rushed past him, dropped to his pudgy knees and wrapped one arm around Masada in a loving hug. "…sada." He kissed her nose. His other arm pulled Diego close. "Deego," he said, and planted his lips on top of the dog's head. Masada remained obedient and sitting, but eagerly licked Aiden's face. The child giggled until he hiccupped.

Sarah stood in the doorway, her face soft from her laughter as she listened to the baby's giggles. Alex's throat tightened as he observed this family scene. He considered his visits with David and Rhonda, who had serious struggles ahead. He marveled because, at this moment, his life felt normal. He regarded Masada as she remained by his side. "Release," he said. Masada made eye contact, bounced up in a little bunny hop, and transformed into a twisting, wagging, fun loving dog. Diego remained next to Kevin, but watched longingly as Masada danced around Aiden and disappeared into the den, with Aiden chattering all the way.

"He's all wound up." Sarah said as she walked over to the refrigerator. "He played in the nursery at the vet center while I went to my spouses' group session." She pulled open the door. "You two want some lunch? I could make sandwiches."

Alex and Kevin looked at one another, shrugged and answered together. "Sure."

They chowed down on the sandwiches as Sarah mixed cookie batter and Alex explained Dave and Rhonda's situation. "Could you go by and talk to her? Maybe invite her to your group?"

"I guess. I could go by after work tomorrow, before I pick up Aiden from my folks. You have classes all day right? But, I'm not sure what to say."

"Just tell her what it was like with us." He swallowed the last bite of his sandwich. "I hope she will already have gone to visit Dave. She said she would."

"She'll go see him, especially if Sarah talks to her." Kevin said as he wiped his mouth. "Thanks for the grub, Sarah." He stood up and looked at Alex. "We'd better get going."

Alex nodded. "I'm going to the treatment court tomorrow after classes and see about volunteering as a mentor. I'm supposed to do community service for my ethics class, so I hope it qualifies." He rose, leaned over, and kissed Sarah. "I'll come by after." He whistled for Masada who came thundering down the hall, Aiden wobbling behind.

Sarah followed the men to the door. "Oh, don't forget we have the last committee meeting for the Veterans Day preparations, tomorrow night at seven. You'll be here for dinner? My folks are coming too. They can ride with us."

"Don't worry, we won't miss it." Kevin said as he pounded Alex on the back. "My man here is the keynote speaker." He smiled and stuck out his chest in exaggeration. "He's going to talk about Masada and explain what service dogs have done for us." He eyed Alex. "You ready for that, bud?"

Alex didn't respond with Kevin's enthusiasm. How was he going to describe what Masada meant to him without crying like a girl?

CHAPTER 42

Unlike the last six months, Alex's reason for arriving early was a normal one, to get a parking space. Until Masada, every time he parked, his nerves were wrapped uptight like a haji at gunpoint, and he had to pry his fingers from the wheel, and yank at his clinging, sweat-soaked t-shirt.

He shut off the ignition and smiled at Masada riding shot gun. "You ready for your first day of classes?" He reached over and ruffled her ears. "Let's go." She scrambled out behind him as he hefted his back pack over his shoulder.

He still scanned the lot. He still scrutinized the students walking the path. He still tensed at shouting, or someone running up from behind. Normal reactions, his counselor said. The responses may never go away. The difference? Alex continually monitored Masada who padded beside him. When his focus dropped down to her, she met his eyes. It was silly to imagine what she might say if she could, but he did. "That's okay, bro. I got your back."

He wanted to skip like a little boy. No more whistling in the dark. No longer alone, he had a team mate. When he arrived at his classroom, a girl of Mid-eastern descent, who usually sat behind him, approached, smiling. Her grey hoodie draped over burnt umber, shoulder length hair. Black cropped leggings clung to her thin calves. "May I pet your dog? She's beautiful." She didn't wait for his answer and leaned down.

"Ma'am, I prefer you didn't. She's working." He studied the girls' attire and verified little could be hidden within the folds.

The girl popped up. "Oh. I'm sorry." She tilted her head to read the words on Masada's vest. "I wasn't paying attention. Now, I see what it says." Her coffee colored skin blushed as she smiled up at him.

Alex returned the smile, relieved she didn't question what kind of work. But he felt compelled to elaborate. "She's a service dog."

The girl's face lit up and her dark eyes danced. "I should have known. There's another dog that comes on campus, His name's Diego. Do you know him?"

"Yes, I know the dog. The guy's a buddy of mine." Kevin had warned him that Masada would be a chick magnet.

She propped her books on her hip. "Are you a veteran, too?"

"I am, Ma'am." He shifted his weight. He didn't want to appear overly friendly, but didn't want to be rude either.

She reached out her hand. "I'm Melita." Her expression softened. "Your friend with Diego, he is very nice."

"Yes, ma'am. His name's Kevin." He waited for her to release his hand. "Mine's Alex." When she let go, he nodded and said," It's nice to meet you." Excusing himself, he pushed past her and headed inside to his seat.

A couple other students eyed Masada, said something to each other, and then took their places. Alex settled into his seat as the professor entered the lecture hall, scanned over the students, and approached the lectern. Masada lay discreetly out of sight at Alex's feet.

As he waited for class to begin Alex's mind drifted. He missed Sarah. He was tired of the separation, tired of staying at the bunkhouse. He wanted to go home, live normal. Since Masada came into his life, his confidence had grown stronger every day. Sarah wanted him home.

And why not? *Just do it.* He played with the idea. His heartbeat fluttered as he considered the possibility. You're never going to know for sure. *Just do it.* He looked down at Masada. Like a sentry, she watched the students passing by in the aisle. Most did not even notice her.

He was going to do it. There. He'd made the decision. He'd talk it over with Sarah tonight, but was sure there would be no opposition from her. He admired his wife's bravery. Maybe she saw something in him he couldn't see. He did feel different. His mind switched to Dave. He'd wondered if Rhonda had visited him.

He tuned in to the professor. "Undergraduate classes will include constitutional law, ethics and integrity, to name a few. All of these will be useful if you select another area of criminal justice besides police work." He shoved his papers back in his briefcase. "Careers in security have increased 20% since 9-11. There are many options to choose from." He zipped up his case. "See you all on Wednesday, and don't forget, there's a test on Friday."

After his last class Alex drove to the treatment court. The information officer loaded him with forms and an application. "We are desperate for volunteers," he said. "The vets really relate to their own. Welcome aboard."

Alex checked the time. He and Masada had time for some PT since Sarah was going to stop by Dave and Rhonda's after work. He headed back to the college and parked by the running track.

He loved running. Even more, he loved running with Masada. She followed him to the grassy area circling the track. Masada stretched with him. "Are you warming up, too?" He chuckled as he patted her. "Come on, let's go."

As usual, a quarter mile into the run, Masada bolted ahead with the grace of a gold medal sprinter. A hundred meters in front she slowed, turned, and waited for him to catch up. Each time she reminded him of his drill sergeant in boot camp who pushed him further than he ever believed he was capable.

They did their five miles and returned to the truck. Masada lapped water from her bowl behind the seat while Alex threw back two bottles of water like he used to do his beer. Another change. He couldn't help feeling proud as he knelt down and wrapped Masada in a huge hug. His eyes watered and his throat tightened. "I love you, girl." He jumped up and swiped at his eyes. "Come on. Let's go home."

When he entered the kitchen, Sarah sat at the kitchen table, feeding Aiden.

"I didn't expect you home this early," he said as he leaned over and kissed the top of her head. He stepped behind Aiden, who banged his little fist on the high chair's tray while Sarah shoveled applesauce in his mouth. "How's my little Devil Pup?" The boy squealed with excitement as his daddy lifted him from his highchair. The child turned his round rosy face to his father and landed an applesauce kiss on his cheek.

"My last appointment cancelled, so I got off early." Sarah reached up and wiped, first the baby's face, and then her husband's. She, too, kissed her husband's cheek. "There you go. You're my Devil dog."

Alex slid Aiden back into his high chair. "So you went to see Rhonda? How did it go?"

"It was strained at first, until I told her all that we'd been through." She spooned more applesauce into Aiden's mouth, who continued to pound on his tray. "I could tell she felt better knowing she wasn't the only one."

"Had she gone to visit Dave?"

"She said she tried, but he wasn't there."

What do you mean, he wasn't there?"

"His Dad posted bail."

"He did? I thought he wasn't going to do that. Did he go to his Dad's?"

"No one knows where he is."

CHAPTER 43

Today was Veterans Day. Alex lay in bed watching Sarah sleep. They had not discussed Dave and Rhonda's situation any further. For Alex, it was too close to home. Although he and Sarah agreed Alex would move back, a simple task of bringing his duffle bag from the bunkhouse, they still faced the unstable facts of their relationship.

They had arrived home from the committee meeting late and exhausted. Alex undressed Aiden and tucked him in while Sarah folded the laundry she'd left in the dryer.

In the bedroom, he watched Sarah undress, dropping her clothes to the floor. Her habit that had sent him into a rage before, made him smile for the first time since he had come home from Iraq. He understood his unreasonable reactions to so many things now, and although he couldn't always stop them, the responses were less intense. The couple climbed into bed, each on their own side, trying to act normal. They lay flat in the dark, staring at the shadows on the ceiling.

Sarah broke the silence. "You're different, Alex. I know you get keyed up at times and when you do, I start to get scared. But now, you unwind just as fast. I am so happy you quit drinking, it really helps." She rose up on her elbow and leaned over him. "I believe everything's going to be okay. I'm so happy you're home."

He pulled her down to him and swallowed her in his arms. "I love you, Sarah." The night had been a closure, a renewal, and a promise, sealed with hungry love making.

Dawn had already pushed away the shadows when Alex woke. He rolled over and peered down at Masada, who had made all this possible. He blinked at the tears that tracked into his hair, and soaked into his pillow. Masada lifted her head and gazed up. *You okay?* Yes, Masada, because of you, I'm okay. He slipped out of bed and dressed in his sweats. He sat on the edge of the garage sale chair Sarah had bought a lifetime ago and shoved on his boots. When had he stopped wearing his boots to bed? He stepped over to the bedside, leaned down, and kissed his wife. Her green eyes fluttered open and he said, "Going for a run. I'll check on Aiden." She smiled, snuggled deeper into the covers, and pulled them over her head.

With a quick peek at Aiden sleeping peacefully in his crib, Alex headed outside. His boots pounded a steady rhythm and he breathed easily as Masada bounded ahead. Dave intruded on his thoughts. He reviewed the hangouts and places his friend frequented. When you're suicidal you don't want to be found. He remembered Dave mentioning a campground above Elsinore just past the Lookout. He had bragged about how he'd taken three cases of beer and camped for the weekend. He'd described it as isolated. At the time, the picture Dave painted appealed to Alex, who was struggling with his own depression. The place had lived in his head during those dark months like an enchanted dream.

A block ahead, Masada, now waiting, stood by a grove of trees, her panting mouth open in a laugh. Today was Veterans Day. He was going to be speaking in front of a crowd, telling everyone how great his life is, because of a dog. Who would believe him? He hardly believed it himself. Just as he jogged up to Masada, she barked playfully, and bolted away. Her golden hair flowed like the shifting sands in the desert at sundown. His heart ached with the love he felt for her. He picked up the pace and caught up to her.

Dave. Alex recalled his own image in the mirror, what seemed a lifetime ago, with his gun to his head. His step faltered and his stomach jerked, because in his mind's eye, now he imagined Dave's face in the mirror. How could Alex's life ever be good as long as one of his comrades was outside the wire?

I hear they're doing great work. I wish every vet could have one. The public defender's words from yesterday floated into Alex's mind between the cadence of his footfall. That was the answer! Every vet should have the opportunity to acquire a service dog. A dog should be part of the exit package, part of the medical benefits. A year waiting list was unacceptable. Marine or not, Alex would have given up the fight if he had had to wait.

Veterans Day. He knew what he was going to say in his speech. He was lucky to be alive. He was only alive because of the dedicated people at K9s For Warriors and the inmates at the Illinois State Correctional Facility. From this point forward he would make it his mission to convince the public and the US government to add a service dog to a veteran's exit package.

His heartbeat raced, not from the run, but from the promise of his new mission. He envisioned a new world, full of thousands of puppy raisers, trainers, and inmates working within hundreds of facilities like K9s For Warriors across the country in order to provide every veteran of every branch of service the opportunity for a service dog.

The Veterans Day ceremony at the Veterans' Center began at ten. Alex arrived early to help set up the chairs and check the sound system. As the keynote speaker, he was scheduled just before the closing ceremonies. Sarah, her folks, and Kevin's were responsible for coordinating the food and refreshments. They expected over five hundred people. Masada even contributed by hanging out with Diego in the nursery with the kids until the celebration began.

The auditorium, decorated in red, white and blue, was full to capacity. A hush filled the room as the color guard marched onto the stage. Chairs scraped as everyone stood and placed their hands on their hearts. The Pledge of Allegiance always sent chills up Alex's arms. The usual shiver tingled his spine when his cell's vibration hummed loudly, interrupting his focus on the proceedings. Sarah turned her head with a questioning look as he pulled the phone from his pocket.

A text. "Dave's in trouble. Please come. Rhonda." He angled the phone for Sarah to read the message. Their eyes met and she nodded.

He whispered to Masada. "Let's go." They scooted past Sarah and Kevin's folks. When Alex reached Kevin, he showed him the text. They slipped out the side door.

As they climbed into the truck, the cell hummed again, and they both checked the screen. "Cops here. Dave has a gun. Please hurry."

The entire sheriff's department surrounded the little house with peeling paint and the abandoned bicycle that still waited by the dead tree. Red lights lit up the SWAT team's grim faces as they crouched behind the squad cars, the dead tree, and the little Honda with the car seats in the back.

"This doesn't look good." Kevin said.

"There's Rhonda." Alex pointed to the police van parked on the corner. "And there's her father-in-law. Where are the kids?" Alex gunned the accelerator, and the truck lurched toward the SWAT team's van. He slammed on the brakes, exhaled the breath he'd been holding, and jumped out. Kevin, Diego and Masada followed.

Rhonda broke from the uniforms who were gathered in a huddle. "Oh, thank God you came. He asked for you, Alex."

"Where are the kids?" He didn't breathe.

Rhonda hung her head and cried uncontrollably. "They're inside."

Alex took a deep breath and placed his hands on her shoulders. "You've got to keep it together, Rhonda." He jostled her. "For the kids."

She gasped and looked up, desperate to see some sign of hope in his eyes. He set his jaw and squinted in determination, "Everything's going to be okay."

He released her and steered her toward Kevin. "Stay with her." He strode away and sought out the SWAT team's commander.

CHAPTER 44

The Commander hunched over a scratched out diagram of the little house's interior. "Alex March, sir."

The commander turned, looked him up and down, then with a steel grip shook Alex's hand. "Commander Delarosa. Thank you for coming, Mr. March. He's asked to talk to you. Can you tell us anything about him?"

"Not any more than you probably already know. He was an excellent Marine. He just got sent home from his second tour after his hummer took a hit. Everyone in his team was killed. He's been diagnosed with Traumatic Brain Injury. He is a great guy, Commander, he just needs help."

"That's what we're going to try to do. Here's the loud speaker. Let him know you're here and you want to talk to him, but he's got to let the kids come out first."

"Yes, sir."

"Delarosa glanced down at Masada, who sat calmly, leaning against Alex's leg. "With all due respect, this is no place for a dog."

Alex's muscles tensed a notch tighter. Masada was all that kept him grounded. Without her, Alex's mind would be back in Iraq, ready to kill the first thing that moved, just to rescue his comrade. He faced Delarosa with a challenging stare. "She's a highly trained service dog, commander. She's trained to deal with stressful situations. She might be the one to deescalate this situation." Delarosa held eye contact and Alex watched the commander's mind quickly calculate the situation.

"I've heard about these dogs." He scrutinized Masada, then nodded in acquiescence. "Carry on."

Alex grabbed the loudspeaker. "Hey, Dave! Semper Fi! How about you let me come in and we'll talk?" Alex's cell vibrated and he pulled it from his pocket. Dave. He handed the loud speaker back to the commander as he tapped the speaker on his cell and said, "Hey jarhead. What are you doing in there? You can't go out like this. Not in front of your kids. Why don't you let them go to their mother? Rhonda's here. She's worried to death."

Delarosa and his captain hovered over the cell. "Aw, Alex. I've scared them again. They're hiding in their room. They won't come out, even for me. You come in."

"I can't do that, buddy. They won't let me come in unless you let the kids go. What do ya say? Rhonda's so worried about them."

Alex cringed as Dave's shouts garbled out of the cell's speaker phone. "Didn't you hear what I said? Everyone's fucking afraid of me. Why do think I'm surrounded by a fucking SWAT team? This isn't how I pictured my life to end. My team-mates did it the supreme way. Why couldn't it have been me, too? Why me?" He wasn't crying because he was a Marine. His hot anger dried his tears.

"I'll tell you what. How about I send Masada and Diego in to bring the kids out?" Alex ignored the piercing looks Delarosa and his captain shot up at him. "Did you know Ricky and Kimberly met them at the house the other day? They loved the dogs. Go ahead, ask them if they remember Masada and Diego." The commander locked eyes when Alex glanced up and acknowledged him, but Alex waved him off. A long silence came from the phone, then a muffled voice, and the rustling sound of movement.

"They said they'd come out if they could see Masada and Diego."

Alex raised his brow to Delarosa, who nod-ded in agreement. "Okay, jarhead. I'm sending Masada and Diego in. You tell the kids to grab hold of their collars so the dogs can take them for a walk. Make a game of it. You can do this, Dave." Alex knew how worthless his buddy felt. Alex hurt, inside and out, with empathy for his friend, yet so grateful he had escaped the torment that now had Dave in their grips. "After they're with their mother, I'll come in. You and I will have a pow wow."

Alex motioned to Kevin, who rushed over with Rhonda by his side. "He's going to let the kids come out." Rhonda slumped, covered her face and sobbed with relief.

"But Ricky and Kimberly are afraid and won't leave the bedroom." Rhonda jerked her head up, her bloodshot eyes rimmed with tears. "We're sending Masada and Diego in to get them."

Rhonda nodded. She looked down at the dogs, her face filled with hope. The thought of all he had put Sarah through popped into Alex's mind. He flushed with shame. Thank God Sarah didn't know he had gone down this far, too. Alex looked at Kevin and nodded toward Rhonda. Kevin read the silent order and reached his arm around her, drawing her close, "It's going to be okay," He said, and handed Diego's leash to Alex.

Alex made eye contact with the dogs and said, "Let's go." He strode across the dried, crisp grass with them in tow. He reached the porch of the little house, unsnapped their leashes, and shouted. "Let the dogs in." The door opened a crack. "Diego, Masada. Inside." They bounded up the steps and entered the dangerous den of uncertainty. Alex's heart twisted as Masada, who had become more important than his own life, disappeared inside. "I'll wait right here, 'til they come out."

Alex reached his arm up and wiped the sweat from his forehead. His mind flashed to that day in Iraq with his comrade, Eddie, and the boy, Yusef. Alex glanced at his sleeve. No blood. No pink mist.

Minutes ticked by. He waited. Police, swat team members, paramedics and firefighters joined in the quiet, tense vigil. Alex's mind flashed to Iraq. He walked point. The silence was loud, like the music from a Jack In the Box just before the clown exploded from its hiding. He waited, expectant. The only sound, his pulse pounding in his ears. The door burst open and Alex jerked.

Dave's muted voice strained out from somewhere inside the little house "Don't shoot. They're coming out."

Alex canceled his reflexive combative crouch, armed with his absent rifle. Masada appeared first. Grown up Kimberly, her small face, too serious for a four year old, marched by the dog's side. Behind, Diego walked hesitantly. Ricky's arms hugged the dog's neck as the toddler teetered alongside, giggling and chattering. Alex dropped to his knees, "Here, Masada, Diego."

The canines made their way to Alex and sat down obediently in from of him. Alex ruffled their fur and smiled at Ricky and Kimberly. "Are the dogs taking you for a walk?" The children turned their heads, looked back into the house's dark interior, then nodded. Kimberly's mouth bent downward and Alex thought she might cry. "Your

Daddy's going to be okay. Masada and I are going to talk to him. Why don't you let Diego take you and Ricky to your mom? See her over there?" He pointed across the yard where Kevin held Rhonda tightly so she wouldn't run to her children.

Kimberly nodded as her lip trembled. "Come on, Deego," she said. She released her grip on Masada's collar and wrapped her little fingers around Diego's, next to her brother's. Alex motioned to Kevin who shouted, "Diego, come."

When the children reached their mother's safe arms, Alex turned, faced the opened door and said, "Masada and I are coming in."

CHAPTER 45

A lex ignored Delarosa's shout, ordering him to wait. The little house held its breath as he stepped inside. Dave sat on the couch that Alex and Kevin had sat, what seemed like a lifetime ago. His elbows on his knees, his hands extended, holding a revolver. He didn't look up.

Alex sank slowly into the recliner across from Dave, Masada took her place alongside and focused on Dave. "Ricky and Kimberly are safe with Rhonda." Alex scratched Masada's ears. "Are you sure you want to do this?

Dave's knee moved up and down to the tapping of his boot heel on the floor.

"I told you. I'm done. The Marine Corps' done with me. Rhonda's and the kids are done. My team's gone and it's my fault." He lifted his head and stared at Alex. His eyes fiery with rage and sunken with lost glory.

"I know, buddy. I know where you're at."

"You don't know!"

Masada stood up in reaction to the increased energy in the room. Dave's knuckles whitened with restraint as he clutched the revolver.

Alex shouted back. "Bull shit! You aren't the only one in the world that's felt like this. I sat in the dark with the cold muzzle against my temple, too. I remember how cold it felt on my skin. How easy it would be. Just like you said, I was done." Alex stood, signaled Masada to stay, and paced the room. "Sarah had left. I couldn't go home, knew I shouldn't go home, for the safety of my wife and kids. At least I had the option to do another tour. Just like you, I saw no way out, but this way."

Dave hung his head. His jaw flexed with the anger boiling inside. "Yeah, so now you are dancing in the street and pigs have wings. Is that it?"

Alex returned to the recliner, sat down on the edge, his own elbows on his knees, and smiled. "Yeah, sure. If you want to buy that story, I'll tell it. Whatever works to get you back under the wire."

"I can't get back. I've tried." Dave's voice rose. "I hate the meds. And the docs want to put me in rehab. How am I gonna take care of my wife and kids if I spend months locked up with shrinks who don't even get it? What I need is a job."

Alex shook his head. "I have to be honest, nothing's easy. But you're not going to get a job locked up or taking a dirt nap."

Dave turned and stared at Alex. Anger flared in his eyes like a wildfire. Alex felt his own heart pounding so loud he was sure Dave could hear it. Dave raised the revolver to his chin, never taking his challenging eyes from Alex's. The crow's feet deepened, his lips only a thin line. Alex held his stare. His buddy's face would haunt him the rest of his days, just like Yusuf's. But he said nothing.

Masada, who still stood, made her move. She covered the distance between the men, and laid her head on Dave's knee. He blinked. Alex read the confusion as it deepened Dave's tortured brow. Alex's own stomach ratcheted tighter with fear for Masada. The service dog placed one paw, onto Dave's lap, and then her other. She sat on her haunches, pressed her shoulder against the warrior's chest, and nuzzled her head in the crux of his neck.

Alex saw the flicker in his eyes. The moment his friend's life changed. The gun dropped to the floor. Dave embraced Masada, his body bent over hers. The warrior sobbed. His red hot tears fell freely and vanished into Masada's fur. She eagerly licked his face, happy her efforts were being rewarded. Dave hugged and kissed her like a Marine coming home from boot camp. Alex's own tears blurred the image before him. Like a magical mist, the man and the dog became an undulating mirage in the desert.

Alex picked up the gun, switched the safety on, and tucked the weapon under his belt as he stood. Dave pulled his attention away from Masada and gazed up. His face flushed with embarrassment. "I don't know what happened here. Whatever it was, I can't believe it. I have never allowed anyone to get this close to me. How did she do that?"

Alex smiled and slapped his buddy on the shoulder. "You have just fallen under the spell of an American Service Dog." Alex extended his hand. "It's going to be okay. No surrender, right?"

Dave weighed the question, rose, and took Alex's extended hand. "I don't know how you did it, but thanks." He pulled Alex to him and gave him a hard hug, then knelt down, and embraced Masada one more time, ruffling her ears and rose. His eyes fell on his M9 under Alex's belt and nodded toward it. "You keep that for me, until I get it together. I don't know how I'm going to do that, but for the first time, I think it might be possible."

Alex grinned as he remembered his experience with Diego. He related the story to Dave. "After that, it was still rough, but I knew there had to be a way. I was lucky I didn't have to wait a year for a dog."

"A year?"

"I'll see if I can push that. No promises. You're required to go through counseling to be approved." Alex studied his buddy's reaction.

Dave grimaced and took a deep breath of resignation. "I'll do it. Who've I been kidding? Just myself. I'll go. I've been resenting you and Kevin since I got home. You guys got it so together. I guess it works for you."

"Hey. Don't think it's easy. Even now. Every day is a struggle. Not one step I've made has been simple, or without consequences. I can't say it gets easier, it's just different, and sometimes even better." Alex crouched down and put his arm around Masada. "I have a teammate now. She watches my back. I'm not alone." His throat tightened as he said the words. He stood up quickly, checking his watch, "I just remembered. I've got a speech to make." He met Dave's eyes. "You know they have to take you back?"

"Yes, I know. I'll do the time." He looked at Masada, and knelt down one more time. "I'll see you when I get out, girl. I owe you, big time." He rose and extended his hand to Alex, again. "Thanks bud. Let's go face the music. You've got a speech to make."

Dave raised his arms, turned and stepped out into the sunshine. The deadly clicks of a dozen firearms filled the air, and aimed red beads on his chest.

THE END

EPILOGUE

Alex lingered as he watched the scene unfold before him. To avoid witnessing their father being taken into custody, Kevin steered Diego and the kids out of sight. The SWAT team lowered their weapons only after the police frisked and cuffed Dave.

Rhonda rushed to her husband's side and embraced him. "Don't worry. We'll work it out. You just get better. The kids and I will be waiting for you when you get out." She kissed his wet, salty face, and wiped his tears away with her palm. He locked eyes with her and said, "I'm sorry for this. I'll make it up to you. I promise."

With an unexpected gentleness, the SWAT commander placed his hand on Dave's arm and said, "We have to hat up and move out." Alex smiled. Delarosa was ex-military.

A warm confidence spread through Alex's veins like a drug. His future was clear. Whatever his career, it would be helping his comrades still outside the wire. That's all he needed to know. That was enough.

Alex checked the time. He could still make the speech. He texted Sarah as he strode to his truck. *Situation defused. All is good. ETA 10.*

Alex approached the podium and the room burst with applause. He breathed deep and stood tall as he faced the crowd. Masada sat by his side at parade rest, chest out, and head held high. They both scanned the audience. It seemed like a dream. Thirty minutes before he had been in another world, reminded of the lowest point of his existence, and how fragile life can be. He waited for the applause to decrease. It ended with a shout from an aged veteran in the back. "Oorah!"

Alex smiled. "Thank you, everyone."

He took another deep breath and pulled out small index cards. His hands trembled. "Since I was asked to speak, I have labored over what to say. I want to say everything that needs be said." His large hands fumbled with the note cards. "So, not to forget anything, and because I am not a speaker, I will read my speech." He glanced up and smiled feebly. The quiet room exuded a respect and an intensity that made his stomach flip-flop.

"Many of you know a veteran like me. One who has come home with no physical injuries and who appears entirely normal. When I set foot on the tarmac, I was relieved to be home, hopeful, and excited to begin my future." He looked up. Heads nodded.

"But stuffed inside my duffle full of dirty underwear, I didn't know I also brought home invisible baggage in the form of nightmares, angry rages, and unreasonable fears. I didn't understand my uncontrollable behavior and worried I was going crazy. I spoke to no one about it, which only isolated me more.

"On home soil I was racked with guilt for my comrades whom I had left behind, and tortured by the horror of the ugliness I'd seen. I felt a separation, isolated from those who have not worn my boots. I wanted to do another tour because in Iraq I was in control.

No one could reach me, not my family, or the civilians for whom I'd fought. When I became engulfed in flashbacks, I feared for my safety, and for the safety of my family. I could no longer face my fellow Marines, my loved ones, or God, without shame and fear."

Alex dared to pull his eyes from his cards. A woman in the third row dabbed her eyes and a young man in the front row sat rigid, his knee jerking up and down. The vet, really just a boy, lifted his Army cap and wiped his brow averting Alex's gaze. His other hand pressed against the nervous knee in an attempt to keep it still.

"This invisible, unspoken burden has a name. PTSD. That's short for Post-Traumatic Stress Disorder. Today it is called The Invisible Disease. In the past it's been known as Battle Fatigue, Shell Shock and Combat Disorder. I call it the Invisible Enemy that the Marine Corps did not train me to fight. It is impossible to fight alone. Yet, for over a year, I attempted to do just that. I failed miserably. My wife left me, my son developed emotional issues, and at my lowest point I tried to end it all by putting a gun to my head."

Sarah jostled Aiden in her arms. If his confession surprised her, she didn't show it. His heart swelled with love. She was Marine-tough.

"But I was lucky. Like the helos thundering in the desert over a desperate firefight, an organization called K9s For Warriors rescued me. Their weapon?" Alex stepped aside, leaving his speech on the podium, and knelt down by Masada. "Meet the most powerful weapon against this devastating, Invisible Enemy, this Invisible Disease. I want you all to meet Masada. She's an American Service Dog.

He swallowed hard. His face constricted to retain his tears, which always threatened to come when he considered Masada's importance to him. It hardly seemed possible, but the silent crowd became even quieter. Only a soft cough murmured from the back of the room, the veteran who had shouted out earlier, wiped an eye.

Alex mustered up his control and stood. "Masada is a service dog. She is my team mate, trained to wake me during a nightmare. She reads my energy and reassures and comforts me when I'm stressed. She's my barometer. If a sound or a smell triggers my brain to react to some nonexistent danger, I check with my team mate. If she is calm, I remain calm." His eyes rested on Masada who returned his gaze. He smiled.

"The Marine Corps trained me to be a killing machine and I have done my job well. I risked my life for my fellow Marines and they risked theirs for mine. Some of those same men died in my arms. I witnessed a small boy explode in front of me. No civilian or family member can ever imagine what images I have to live with. Nor do I want them to. When I am not with my comrades, I am alone with my memories. But all I have to do is look at Masada. She assures me that no matter what I have seen, or what I have done, she accepts me.

"I guess you could say Masada is a trained, caring machine. She has gone through eighteen months of intensive training and she, too, does her job well. She has saved me from jumping over an emotional ledge where there is no return.

Today she performed another miracle. She rescued a fellow Marine from surrendering to this Invisible Enemy. Do you know how she did it? She loved him at his worst. She didn't care what he had done in the past, what he couldn't do now. She just loved him and kissed his face. She melted his anger, cooled his fear, and smothered his depression. If I don't get anything else across to you folks today, I want you to go home knowing these service dogs work miracles.

"But you need to know the real crisis. The waiting list to acquire a service dog is over a year long. The need and demand for these miracle workers is monumental. Every hour a veteran commits suicide. As I stand before you today, I am pledging to change that. I envision a service dog as part of every veteran's exit package. I will fight for every veteran, who is still lost outside the wire and do everything in my power to bring him home.

"Please help me and pledge your support. Thank you."

The quiet crowd exploded in applause. Chairs scraped and the inspired audience stood. The room filled with energy as they continued to clap even louder.

Embarrassed, Alex glanced down at Masada. "Let's go." The new team crossed the stage and made their way back to Sarah and Aiden.

Sarah stood and kissed her Marine. "Welcome home."

He was under the wire.

"Ooh Rah."

"War is an ugly thing, but it is not the ugliest of things. The decayed and degraded state of moral and patriotic feeling which thinks that nothing is worth war is much worse. A man who has nothing for which he is willing to fight, nothing he cares about more than his own personal safety, is a miserable creature who has no chance of being free, unless made so by the exertions of better men than himself."

– John Stuart Mill

ABOUT THE AUTHOR

After the death of Judy Howard's husband in 2004, Judy became inspired to pursue writing and traveling.

Her first book, a memoir titled, COAST TO COAST WITH A CAT AND A GHOST, an inspirational and uplifting account of how to survive after the death of a loved one.

Judy Howard's second book,, GOING HOME WITH A CAT AND A GHOST, is a romantic mystery appealing to everyone in the second half of their life who have asked themselves, "What if?" Even in this work of fiction, Judy Howard delivers to the reader a message about how to rise above life's tragedies.

Once again, in the author's third book, MASADA'S MARINE, the uplifting message of overcoming life's dramatic hurdles is delivered. Howard draws the reader into the life of a Marine Corps veteran who struggles with PTSD when he comes home from Iraq and, also, into the life a dog named Masada, who becomes a service dog for the wounded warrior.

Judy Howard began a dog grooming career at the age of eleven and still works part time as a groomer. When Judy and her cat, Sportster, are not traveling in their Winnebago motorhome they reside in Sun City, California.

Judy Howard is currently creating the second book in The Masada Series.

CONTACT JUDY HOWARD AT:

Her website: WWW.JudyHowardPublishing.com

Her e-mail: jhoward1935@gmail.com

CHECK OUT OTHER BOOKS BY JUDY HOWARD

COAST TO COAST WITH A CAT AND A GHOST

When her husband of 25 years passes away, Judy Howard is faced with confusing feelings and an overwhelming sense of loss. Accompanied by her cat, Sportster, and a stuffed doll whose uncanny and somewhat unsettling resemblance to her late husband leads to her calling it Jack Incarnate, Howard takes to the road on an RV trip from her home on California's Pacific coast to Florida's Atlantic. And what happens next surprises even her.

A touching, poignant, and empowering journey of discovery—and self-discovery, Howard's debut is an inspiring road story full of surprises and universal truths. Beginning with a sobering and altogether real accounting of death, the author quickly regains her footing and seizes her life with courage and gusto. The antics of Sportster, in addition to Jack Incarnate's needling comments, add lightness and humor while she experiences the challenges and fears, and yet wonderful discoveries of a road trip. From the unsettling circumstances of leaving everything familiar behind, to the challenge of crossing Lake Pontchartrain, to dealing with the spirit of Jack and seeing, for the first time, the Atlantic Ocean – this middle-aged bildungsroman clarifies her life's path, and in the end, comes to terms with her deep love for Jack, despite the abuse that was a part of their relationship and emerges a stronger woman for it.

Weaving an emotionally charged narrative with humorous anecdotes and a unique perspective on life, Howard's odyssey of overcoming grief to find her true self is, in essence, the story of each of us. Full of heart and a budding fearlessness, this quintessential road trip delivers on every level, as moving and fulfilling as it is entertaining. Powerfully written and eloquently understated, *Coast to Coast with a Cat and a Ghost* is the most surprising and satisfying memoir in recent memory.

GOING HOME WITH A CAT AND A GHOST

This is a fictional story about life's complexities for Judy Howard: Liberated enough to drive forward in her RV, yet still imprisoned by her 40 year old past when she was drugged, raped, and had an illegal abortion.

Judy Howard, a typical sixteen year old growing up in the Midwest in 1965, is naïve and shy, with a forbidden James Dean crush on the high school's "bad boy" named Brad. As Judy and Brad flirt with their desires for one another, life is easy, until Judy is drugged and date raped on a Saturday night in the roller rink parking lot. Her bad boy crush, Brad, rescues her after the crime and arranges for an illegal abortion.

The results changed their lives forever. The drug preventing Judy from knowing her attacker causes her to live in fear. The guilt of the abortion drives her to accept a college offer in California. Judy flees to the west coast in an attempt to escape her shame, guilt and fear, but is unable to leave her nightmares and regrets in Illinois. She marries and makes a life for herself for forty years but is haunted by memories of Brad, nightmares of the rape and constant regrets, and questions of "What if..?"

The opportunity to confront her lifelong question of "What if..?" comes when her husband dies and Brad invites her to their 40th high school reunion. Gathering up her shaky courage, Judy heads home to face her past...and who knows? – Her future?

She makes the trip in her motorhome, which she's named The Wizard of Winnebago, accompanied by Sportster, her cat, and a life-sized doll she calls Cowboy Jack, who rides shotgun. The odyssey is a discovery of Route 66 but also a deep examination of her feelings and about the woman she has become since she snuggled in the backseat of Brad's 57 Chevy.

Brad has lived the last four decades married only to the police force, obsessed with investigating and capturing the biggest drug dealer in the Midwest, called Pit Bull. Brad, too, has lived his life with regrets and guilt, always tortured with his own "What ifs?" When he invites Judy to the reunion his mind is made up. He will not waste another moment wondering. He is going to pursue the love of his life and end his doubts.

As Judy progresses toward Springfield and Brad nears closing the biggest case of his career, they are both confronted with the past when Pit Bull threatens to put an end, not only to the mysteries of the past, but their future.

51268307R00208

Made in the USA
San Bernardino, CA
17 July 2017